SUCCESSFUL FUNDRAISING
A Practical Guide

David Warwick

BADGER PUBLISHING

This book is dedicated to my wife Rosemary.

Acknowledgments we are grateful to the Institute of Charity Fundraising Managers for permission to reprint the pamphlet *Code of Practice for Fundraising in Schools* and to Margaret James for her help in the typing of this manuscript.

ISBN   1 872 72819 7
First published 1991

Contents

The aim of this guide is to provide a concise, simple introduction to fund raising. Whilst every effort has been made to ensure the information in this guide is correct at the time of going to press, neither the authors nor the publishers can accept any liability for any errors or omissions, nor can they accept responsibility with regard to the standing of any organisation mentioned in section 6 of the guide. This guide does not attempt to give legal advice in particular cases. Where reference has been made to legal matters such as the law on the sale of alcohol or the obtaining of an official consent, this is by way of illustration only and specific legal advice should always be sought where appropriate.

This only is charity, to do all,
all that we can.

John Donne

Some Thoughts and Facts About Charities ———————

There are now in Britain approximately 170,000 different charities registered with the Charity Commissioners. It is likely that a proportion of them have ceased operating some years ago, since there has never been a full-scale attempt to update the register. These charities range from the nationally and internationally known to small groups such as the registered charity in Islington that works to achieve the neutering of dogs.

A charity is defined as a body with charitable objectives that are justifiably so in law. The organisation needs to be working towards relief of poverty, educational or religious objectives or some other beneficial purpose within society. Those seeking charitable status should look to be registered with the Charity Commissioners. Members of the public have the right to request from the Commissioners the following information:

- the name of the charity
- its constitution and objectives
- the approximate annual income raised
- the name and address of the person in the group who can be contacted with enquiries

Personal searches of the records of a charity can be made at the Charity Commission (Registration Division), St Alban's House, 57–60 Haymarket, London SW1 (071-216-8773).

In a recent survey of attitudes to charities and fundraising, 49 per cent of those questioned were convinced that they gave as much as they could from their earnings. Eighty-nine per cent said they thought the government should do more to support the work of charities.

Introduction

Is it your intention or responsibility to raise useful sums of money for charity, preferably in an inventive and original way? Are you bored by the idea of yet another sponsored event? Can you barely bring yourself to face one more jumble sale, with that enormous heap of odorous unsold jumble left at the end? If that is your situation or your outlook, or if you merely want to consider some rather more unusual events, this book may have just the idea for you.

The fact must be faced that there are now more groups than ever – school Parent–Teacher Associations (PTAs), youth clubs and similar groups, charities of all kinds – that compete as fundraisers. It is standard and necessary practice, especially during the summer months, to check the date and time with great care to minimise the number of other events likely to clash with your own elaborately prepared occasion. The saddest way for your Summer Fête to fail is due to poor summer weather; the second saddest is because two or three other fêtes are taking place just down the road. Essentially, what you need are good ideas and an original approach to make your event strikingly different. *Successful Fundraising* aims to help you to achieve just that. Ralph Waldo Emerson once wrote 'Philanthropies and charities have a certain air of quackery.' You must avoid the fraudulent and charlatan at all costs, but the compelling eccentricity of the quack-doctor and his or her alleged flair with an audience will serve you well.

This book is not designed for use by large organisations or anyone whose view of fundraising is coloured by six- or seven-figure sums. It is designed for smaller groups and the amateur; indeed, even for people who find themselves attempting to fundraise for the first time. Their work could be considered as practical philanthropy. Above all else, *Successful Fundraising* seeks to be of practical use. Once one of the suggestions for fundraising has been accepted, the materials are then provided for planning the event, including the budget, arranging the publicity and afterwards evaluating the success or failure of the result. Some of the ideas are self-explanatory through their title, but in each case the idea is briefly explained and advice is then given. The guide at the end of each activity shows how costly, elaborate and potentially profitable the event is. While success can never be guaranteed, in each case – assuming efficient organisation – success is attainable.

It was Lord Samuel who expressed the opinion that charitable work only deals with symptoms rather than causes. Even a dedicated and determined fundraiser may want to agree. Nonetheless, what can be achieved should not be underestimated. The largest-scale fundraising may fail entirely to bring about a cure for disease: it may only ease some of the massive suffering that follows a famine or an earthquake. Closer to home and on a smaller scale, though, it may solve the entire problem, so that the church has its new roof or the school its extension. The power of the amateur fundraisers should not be underestimated. It is for that band of amateurs that this book is intended.

Section 1
Some Winning Ideas
for Fundraisers

This section provides a range of different ideas and activities from the well-established, standard fundraising events. We all know about Jumble Sales, Sponsored Walks, Summer Fêtes and Autumn Fairs. What is of real interest to the fundraiser is the idea that has novelty and originality on its side. A few of the ideas suggested are really unusual and most are sufficiently out of the ordinary to offer the potential for publicity that the fundraiser needs. There are two main ways of using this section:

- browse through the ideas and select three or four new ones to present at your next committee meeting;
- use the guide at the end of each activity to identify the type of event you'd like to set up and then look only at those that meet your requirements.

A brief explanation is made for each idea to enable the preparations for each event to begin. Some questions have been deliberately left unanswered, though, since it is essential that each event bears the stamp of its organisers.

There is a section for planning notes as well as a space to start some form of *post mortem*. It will stand you in good stead if you work out why your event succeeded or how it could have been improved! (See also Section 7: *Post-mortem Time*.)

Assessing the Potential of a Fundraising Idea ——————

At the end of each activity is given a quick guide to enable you to assess the idea at a glance.

Costs

- **Low:** the event may involve you in no preparatory cost at all and in any case will be a low-risk venture. Even allowing for a certain amount of advance publicity, the total cost should not exceed £50.
- **Moderate:** this category indicates moderate costs in setting up the event. Allow for up to £100.
- **High:** there is a greater risk here of the fundraiser's ultimate disaster – actually losing money. Total costs are likely to exceed £100.

Organisation

- **Simple:** the event is extremely simple to prepare, requiring few people and relatively little time.
- **Moderate:** a fair amount of preparation will be necessary.
- **Considerable:** this is an elaborate event that will call for a considerable amount of advance planning.

Profit

- **Low:** this is not likely to be a huge money-spinner.
- **Moderate:** there is the clear potential with this event for you to achieve a three-figure sum as your profit.
- **High:** properly organised, your fundraising event could bring a profit in excess of £1000.

Author's Note: The perfect fundraising event – low cost, simple organisation and high profit – will not, I am sorry to say, be found in these pages. If you have identified one, please write by return post!

List of Fundraising Ideas

ANTIQUES ROADSHOW

Television has already done much of the advance publicity for you for this type of event, so adopt what is recognisably a similar format. The trickiest part will be finding your tame expert or experts, but there should be candidates amongst the more up-market antique shops in your area. Agree a suitably-worded safeguard clause in case something is undervalued and the owner subsequently protests.

Charge a realistic admission rate, so that the 'consultation fee' can be reasonable. People should then be prepared to bring along several items to be assessed. You will need a generous deal with your expert to be able to make sufficient profit, so offer to publicise his or her business. You may wish to consider linking this event with a sale or auction of some of the items at a later date.

Cost: Moderate
Organisation: Considerable
Profit: Moderate

Date tried	
Target profit	£
Profit (actual)	£

Very successful   worthwhile   unsucessful

Notes/Comments

– ATHONS

Exactly what sort of -athon you decide on is important, and preferably it should be a reasonably unusual-athon. Many kinds have been tried with good success: spellathons, knitathons, readathons, even bounce-athons (see BOUNCING). Perhaps, though, you can find a genuinely original idea to use.

Sponsorship tends to be involved with this activity, but bear in mind that you have a captive audience, which is by definition likely to be around for some while. You may therefore wish to make the provision of refreshments a quite major part of the actual fundraising (see COFFEE MORNINGS, CRECHE, ICE CREAM/YOGURT/MILK SHAKES, REFRESHMENTS STALL/CAFÉ).

Cost: Low
Organisation: Moderate
Profit: Moderate

Date tried	
Target profit	£
Profit (actual)	£

Very successful   worthwhile   unsuccessful

Notes/Comments

AUCTION OF PROMISES/PLEDGES

This is a thoroughly good fundraiser and should also provide a most entertaining and lively afternoon or evening. You do need, though, some really interesting, unusual and valuable lots to be donated (you may wish to encourage a better response through a 50/50 arrangement), so here are a few ideas to prompt people with. They could offer, for example:

- use of a trailer for the weekend
- three - 30 minute sessions on a sunbed
- loan of a time-share property
- taxi for four people (up to 100 miles)
- one ton of well-rotted farm manure
- a flight in a hot air balloon
- 3 hours of golf tuition from a professional coach
- a 3-course vegetarian meal for six, brought to your home (and served, if wished)
- use of 16-foot scaffold tower for two weeks
- a class in relaxation for up to four people
- a watercolour painting of your own home by a professional painter
- a room (up to 15' x 15') (4.6 x 4.6 metres) decorated for you (your own materials)

and dozens more, of course.

The important thing to remember is that nobody can claim to be unable to offer anything. Time provided to babysit, do gardening, knit garments, etc., is as popular as any other item. Lots that represent professional time (e.g. a solicitor offers to draw up a pair of wills) have considerable financial value. As with all auctions, the compiling of the catalogue is time-consuming and has to be done to a tight deadline. The wonderful advantage of this type of auction is not being left with unsold storage heaters and enormous, unappealing wardrobes. Many potential donors will need to be given examples of the type of offer that could be made. It is a good idea to offer a small prize for the most unusual pledge received. The event can be turned into more of a social occasion by combining it with a supper or buffet. If at all possible, do obtain the services of a professional auctioneer.

Cost: Moderate
Organisation: Considerable
Profit: High

Date tried

Target profit   £

Profit (actual)   £

Very successful   worthwhile   unsuccessful

Notes/Comments

BABYSITTING

This may not be an idea to set the pulse racing perhaps, nor a high-scorer for originality. What is easily overlooked, though, is the potential for some useful fundraising from organised group provision of this much-needed service.

Rates are currently an absolute minimum of £1 per hour or part-hour, normally with extra required from late-returners. Therefore, if on a given evening six members of your organisation babysit for an average of three hours, at the very least £18 is pitched into the coffers at the end of the sessions. It is easy to see how quite worthwhile sums can accumulate. If the children will co-operate they could be encouraged to work (drawing posters etc.) for the group!

Look carefully at those who are prepared to take part. You could hold an induction session for them and issue a card to indicate that some vetting has taken place. This indication that it is official and in aid of your very worthwhile cause could also add a bit to your hourly rate. Ideally, one person will take the task of acting as contact, the maker of bookings and general organiser.

Cost: Low
Organisation: Moderate
Profit: Moderate

Date tried

Target profit £

Profit (actual) £

Very successful   worthwhile   unsuccessful

Notes/Comments

BADGES

This can operate in one of three ways:

1. You purchase badges in bulk at a discount and then re-sell them. This is an obvious gamble with only very limited profits.

 Cost: High
 Organisation: Simple
 Profit: Low

2. You design a badge or badges and have them produced commercially – a little more promising if you have good ideas, design sense and have assessed the market accurately.

 Cost: Moderate
 Organisation: Moderate
 Profit: Low

3. By far the best approach is to buy your own badge-making machine and then produce exactly the range and quantity that you believe will be required. The initial outlay will be quite high (current prices are £400 approximately). Even so, the potential profit is sufficient at 30p or even 40p per badge that the machine can pay for itself quite quickly. See Section 6: *Useful Addresses*.

Remember also that there is the potential to hire out your machine to others.

 Cost: High
 Organisation: Considerable
 Profit: High

Date tried

Target profit   £

Profit (actual)   £

Very successful   worthwhile   unsuccessful

Notes/Comments

BAGS

Mainly for schools

There are several similar types of these waterproof nylon bags available, which have widespread appeal as a versatile, general-purpose kit-bag. They normally have hand grips and a shoulder strap, two or more zip pockets and are suitably reinforced. It is possible to have the name of a school or organisation printed on them at no extra cost (but remember that if you do run into difficulties selling them, having the name or crest on *all* of them could be a disadvantage).

You need a large group of potential customers – say a school of 800+ pupils – for this to raise a significant sum. One firm offers discount in the form of 'free' books (which may not be how you would prefer your profit to arrive). There is generally a minimum number to be ordered, for example 30 bags. It is the kind of activity that may well run very satisfactorily for six months or so, but selling the *second* batch of bags tends to be much harder.

Cost: Low
Organisation: Simple
Profit: Low

Date tried

Target profit   £

Profit (actual)   £

Very successful   worthwhile   unsuccessful

Notes/Comments

BARN DANCE

With the demise of ballroom dancing and the fact that many find disco dancing unchallenging and unrewarding, the barn dance has enjoyed something of a revival in recent years. If you are looking for an event where, as long as you have a good band and caller, people are virtually bound to join in with the fun, this is for you.

Very little advice is needed, surely, on how to organise a barn dance. One decision is necessary, though: how far like an authentic barn dance do you wish to make your venue? My advice would be that you do try to achieve a reasonably appropriate atmosphere.

Cost: Moderate
Organisation: Considerable
Profit: Moderate

Date tried	
Target profit	£
Profit (actual)	£

Very successful   worthwhile   unsuccessful

Notes/Comments

BED-PUSH RACE

If your intention is to do something really quite silly in order to raise money, putting wheels onto beds and racing them compares well with most other ideas. It has an appeal both to the public and the media because it combines the elements of a race with the nonsense of nightgowns, nightcaps and converted beds. The beds will need a good, solid set of wheels or they will not complete the first lap.

The course should be between 2–10 miles (3–16 kms) in total length and, if any use of public roads is planned, full consultation with the local police will be necessary. Indeed, unless you have thought out very carefully the business of overtaking, official consent for this activity may not be forthcoming. Spectators will be attracted, so crowd control must be considered very carefully. Collections – using buckets, blankets or both – can be most successful if your publicity has been effective and the sun shines.

Some similar silly race ideas to consider include the Pram Race, Lawn Mower Race, Bath Tub Race. In each case, though, safety must be absolutely paramount. It is far better to use another idea than risk injury to anyone, fundraiser or spectator.

Cost: Low
Organisation: Considerable
Profit: Moderate

Date tried

Target profit   £

Profit (actual)   £

Very successful   worthwhile   unsuccessful

Notes/Comments

BINDING/LAMINATING SERVICE

... or photocopying or editing or copy-typing ... There is a wide range of secretarial and technical services that are in good demand. Yet how many homes, small companies or village schools, for example, possess their own ring-binding machine or laminator? You could provide this valuable service.

For around £200 you can purchase either of the above machines (see Section 6: *Useful Addresses*), or for even less than that if you are able to reclaim the VAT. For that outlay you have a machine that can bind or laminate thousands of items, so it has the potential to pay for itself quite quickly.

The main challenge is how to become sufficiently well known. Word of mouth will help considerably, and you can always laminate your own advertising copy!

Cost: High
Organisation: Simple
Profit: Moderate

Date tried	
Target profit	£
Profit (actual)	£

Very successful   worthwhile   unsuccessful

Notes/Comments

BINGO

'Surely,' you say to yourself, 'he's not going to recommend Bingo, of all things.' In its previous incarnations as Housey-Housey and Lotto it died terrible deaths, but Bingo does consistently bring in the customers and is worth considering as a fundraising event. The most important point with this activity is to run it with clockwork regularity all through the year, so your supporters know that if it's Monday, it must be Bingo.

The profits may not appear all that sensational. An organisation I knew well ran a regular Monday evening Bingo session for the local community which happened to consist of a large proportion of elderly people, a small quota of public transport and a 2.5 mile (4km) walk to the nearest 'professional' Bingo centre. They only raised £25–30 per night. Even so, because they operated come hailstorm or hurricane right through the year, you may not need your calculator to see that they were managing a profit of around £1300 to £1600 each year at the same time as providing a very enjoyable amenity for local people. One of the advantages is that once you have the basic equipment – a really good caller is a vital component – the costs are minimal.

Cost: Moderate
Organisation: Moderate
Profit: High

Date tried	
Target profit	£
Profit (actual)	£

Very successful   worthwhile   unsuccessful

Notes/Comments

BLOCK BOOKINGS

This is the simplest of ideas, but it can produce a reasonable profit. Most theatres, concert halls and similar organisations allow free tickets or reduced prices for large bookings. You arrange the outing, make the booking, everyone in your group agrees to pay the ordinary price and the fundraising account receives the difference. If you have the use of a minibus to provide transport as well, the potential for the occasion becomes even greater.

Ensure, though, that you have the money in early for the tickets or somebody will be left with a sizeable, if probably short-term, debt. This is not a huge fundraiser, but over a period of time it can be well worth doing.

Cost: Low
Organisation: Simple
Profit: Low

Date tried	
Target profit	£
Profit (actual)	£

Very successful   worthwhile   unsuccessful

Notes/Comments

BOOKSHOP

New or second-hand books always make a colourful display and have good potential for profitmaking. You can boost your stock if members of your group and supporters are prepared to donate free or much reduced books acquired through book club membership. Try to open at a regular time so that, for example, it becomes known that *every* Saturday morning between ten and twelve your bookshop will be operating. You can vary the activity through the occasional 'Book Fair' involving other contributors, or perhaps setting up a book-signing session or an event specialising in books on a particular theme (e.g. sports).

Cost: Low
Organisation: Moderate
Profit: Moderate

Date tried	
Target profit	£
Profit (actual)	£

Very successful   worthwhile   unsuccessful

Notes/Comments

BOUNCING!

While in theory this is an activity for anyone of any age with excess energy, bouncing will mainly appeal to the under-10s. Quite simply, a large inflatable object – a castle and 'Mr Bounce the Dragon' are two of the available examples – is hired and participants either pay to use it (profit: Low) or are sponsored to use it (profit: High). See Section 6: *Useful Addresses*.

Cost: Moderate
Organisation: Simple
Profit: See above

Date tried	
Target profit	£
Profit (actual)	£

Very successful   worthwhile   unsuccessful

Notes/Comments

BRAINS TRUST

This may not sound like an exciting evening or a significant fundraiser, but with one or two well-known panellists and perhaps two other good speakers of local repute, some lively questions and well-organised refreshments, it can result in a highly successful occasion. The title 'Brains Trust' is hardly calculated to excite, though. Instead, call it something like 'Question Time', 'Ask the Experts' or 'Any Questions'.

Cost: Moderate
Organisation: Considerable
Profit: Low

Date tried	
Target profit	£
Profit (actual)	£

Very successful   worthwhile   unsuccessful

Notes/Comments

BRING AND BUY

I confess. This is a hoary old-stager, but it should not be under-rated. Its success is based on the fact that people will actually do both. Either the bringing or the buying would suffice to support the event and the organisation, but it is not all that uncommon for people even to bring and buy back the same item! Anything that generates that measure of enthusiasm must be worth considering.

Above all else, look to achieve a pleasant atmosphere. This may mean someone at the door to welcome the arrivals, or some quiet and preferably inoffensive music in the background to break the silence in the early minutes. Neither of these should cost you any extra. If you are providing coffee, real ground coffee can be sold at a good profit and does convey a very different message from the cheapest bulk-purchase instant stuff from the hypermarket. Those attending will be accustomed to the idea of paying a small admission fee for such events.

Cost: Low
Organisation: Moderate
Profit: Moderate

Date tried

Target profit   £

Profit (actual)   £

Very successful   worthwhile   unsuccessful

Notes/Comments

BUSKING

It is possible to earn good sums in a day or less if the performers are good enough. Consider using a group of people who rotate their acts and bear in mind that jugglers, fire-eaters and magicians can be just as successful as musical performers.

There are sites where busking is officially permitted and where you will need to book a time when you may perform. This permit is obtainable through the local authority. Otherwise, specific permission must be sought and received.

Cost: Low
Organisation: Simple
Profit: Moderate

Date tried	
Target profit	£
Profit (actual)	£

Very successful   worthwhile   unsuccessful

Notes/Comments

CALENDARS

Calendars can provide excellent publicity for your organisation if you have a minimum of six good quality, black-and-white photographs of the activities of the past year (copies of local press pictures are reasonable in price, but check the editor's willingness for them to be reproduced). Otherwise, a variety of attractive pictures – ideally, with a common theme – will do. Include a brief caption, one or two months to that page, space for 'NOTES' to be jotted, a short quotation for each page (humorous or at least reasonably thought-provoking). They are best spirally bound with a hanging attachment. Go for as good quality paper or card as possible: it adds greatly to the effect. Priced at around £2 per calender, profits should begin to accrue after roughly 150 have been sold.

Cost: High
Organisation: Moderate
Profit: Moderate

Date tried	
Target profit	£
Profit (actual)	£

Very successful   worthwhile   unsuccessful

Notes/Comments

CARDS AND NOTELETS

Some of the preparatory work has been carried out for you since many people are attuned to buying cards and notelets to support the large charities that already produce their own. This competition means, though, that your goods must be distinctive and represent good value.

Ideally, use local scenes, material that reflects your organisation and its work or locally-produced designs. Don't try for too many different designs or card sizes. Similarly, colour tends to add considerably to the cost. An attractive black-and-white sketch of the local church will sell just as well. If you can, have on offer one version that is plain inside or carries no more that a 'Best Wishes' greeting and one that is specifically linked to Christmas. Sadly, because the commercial side to Christmas gets under way in late August these days, you will need to have the latter designs ready long in advance of December 25th.

Cost: Moderate
Organisation: Moderate
Profit: Moderate

Date tried	
Target profit	£
Profit (actual)	£

Very successful   worthwhile   unsuccessful

Notes/Comments

CAROL SINGING

Carol singing must never be a bunch of dissonant warblers fresh from the pub making a mockery of 'Good King Wenceslas'. Nobody needs that, least of all at Christmas time. If you intend to undertake carol singing to raise funds, it means several rehearsals and a carefully prepared repertoire. At least half of you need to be musically capable, or the group would do better to stay silent.

Because of the nature of the activity, you should make it clear that your group represents a good cause and that some of the proceeds will go to possibly a third world or children's charity.

Cost: Low
Organisation: Moderate
Profit: Moderate

Date tried	
Target profit	£
Profit (actual)	£

Very successful   worthwhile   unsuccessful

Notes/Comments

CAR RALLY

By law you are not permitted to race on the public highways – and that includes car rallies where there is a time factor built into the event. This needs to be stressed, therefore, to any of the participants who have seen film footage of the Monte Carlo and other rallies and fancy their chances. Any problems regarding the organisation of your rally – including matters of legality – should be directed to the RAC who has authority to supervise such an activity.

If you have not tried this before, it is well worth consulting with someone who has. Your clues must not be too cryptic, unless, that is, you actually want to leave dozens of innocent people stranded, scattered and lost all around the countryside. Make sure also that you remove any markers, symbols and clues as soon as it is all over. The emphasis is best placed on a good social occasion, rather than trying to make large sums in profit.

Cost: Low
Organisation: Considerable
Profit: Low

Date tried

Target profit   £

Profit (actual)   £

Very successful   worthwhile   unsuccessful

Notes/Comments

CELEBRITY CAST-OFFS

Such is our national obsession with 'celebrities' and 'stars' that even that young lad fresh out of theatre school who sits in a studio as a link-man on local radio somehow becomes regarded as *famous*. This method of achieving surprisingly large sums of money depends on the organisers contacting celebrities and asking them to donate an item of clothing or some other possession which can then be auctioned or sold.

Very elaborate preparation is needed for this, but you will be astonished at how much people will pay for a well-known tennis player's sweat-bands or a pop-star's still warm T-shirt. Some of the items may actually be useful (e.g. a golf-ball, a racket cover or an autographed LP) but the appeal of this event, of course, is in the novelty of the goods.

Cost: Moderate
Organisation: Considerable
Profit: High

Date tried	
Target profit	£
Profit (actual)	£

Very successful   worthwhile   unsuccessful

Notes/Comments

CHEESE AND WINE PARTY

Before you point out that this is hardly an original idea, remember that your approach to it could be. Far too often these events offer nothing more sociable than the cheapest, mildest and least acceptable cheddar the cash-and-carry could provide, with glasses of wine to match – the sort of toxic stuff that gets wine-growers a bad name.

It is, however, possible to provide something rather more appealing while keeping to reasonable prices and making a fair profit. It should be possible to negotiate a discount of at least 5 per cent if you buy the wine by the case – and with some retailers that could even apply for a mixed case.

You may also wish to use an 'expert'; to introduce your wines or your cheeses, or both. If you haven't a suitable contact, one of the local off-licences or supermarkets might be able to help.

Cost: High
Organisation: Moderate
Profit: Moderate

Date tried	
Target profit	£
Profit (actual)	£

Very successful   worthwhile   unsuccessful

Notes/Comments

CHRISTMAS CARDS

Start with a design competition with perhaps small prizes for the winners. Then make your decision: do you attempt to produce your cards through desk-top publishing methods or use of a photocopier or do you have the design(s) commercially produced? (See Section 6: *Useful Addresses* if you are interested in the latter approach.) Printing will be expensive unless you order in excess of 1000 copies of each design!

The competition will need to be arranged as early as February or March if you are to have the cards ready for sale at the necessary time. Remember that unfortunately the Christmas catalogues from charities now arrive in late August or early September, so you are wasting your and other people's time if your cards, however good they may be, come rolling off the presses on 3rd December.

Do not attempt to provide too great a range of card designs, but it does help to have some variety, if only because people like to buy a pack of different cards. Keep the unsold cards and don't despair, for they will probably sell successfully alongside the new ones next year!

Cost: High
Organisation: Moderate
Profit: Moderate

Date tried	
Target profit	£
Profit (actual)	£

Very successful   worthwhile   unsuccessful

Notes/Comments

CHRISTMAS DECORATIONS

For many people individual, hand-made decorations at Christmas are infinitely preferable to the mass-produced kind. Most people, though, do not have the time to make them. As a result a promising gap in the market emerges for you to fill.

You are recommended *not* to try producing Christmas wreaths in quantity. They are both time-consuming and fiddly. Small decorations for the table are a more promising area. The basic items needed are a block of wood, some oasis, a small spray of foliage, a candle, glue, glitter and spray-paint. Other simple but effective ideas include decorated cones and a pine bough hung with a variety of tinsels and baubles. This is an extremely labour-intensive activity, but it is possible to make a good sum in a very short time.

Cost: Moderate
Organisation: Considerable
Profit: Moderate

Date tried	
Target profit	£
Profit (actual)	£

Very successful   worthwhile   unsuccessful

Notes/Comments

COFFEE MORNINGS _____

The humble coffee morning should not be underestimated as a raiser both of funds and the level of interest in your organisation. One approach is to run a series of these mornings with a variety of themes (see GAMES EVENING, CRAFT AND PET SHOW, TALENT SHOWS, ANTIQUES ROADSHOW). Do serve decent coffee, though. The cheapest, most acrid stuff on the market will do little for the reputation of your events. Proper ground coffee does reduce the profit margin slightly, but it will bring in more customers. I know of a school that has no trouble in attracting supply teachers because of the exceptionally good cup of coffee available in the staffroom at breaktime.

Cost: Low
Organisation: Simple
Profit: Low

Date tried

Target profit   £

Profit (actual)   £

Very successful   worthwhile   unsuccessful

Notes/Comments

COINS, A MILE OF (OR KILOMETRE?) _____

This is slightly more interesting than the standard method for collecting loose change, whereby a huge jar is on display and, once filled to the brim, is smashed into small pieces by some local celebrity. You simply aim to collect and display a mile of coins. It is visually more intriguing, possible to see the target being approached and a good deal more lucrative than you would expect.

If you decide on 2p pieces one mile (1.6 kms) will produce approximately £600. Using 5p pieces instead will give you a total of around £2200. It is worth setting them out on display whenever you hold another event, thereby hinting broadly that they might add a few yards (metres).

Cost: Low
Organisation: Simple
Profit: Moderate

Date tried	
Target profit	£
Profit (actual)	£

Very successful   **worthwhile**   **unsuccessful**

Notes/Comments

COME RACING!

'All the fun of the racecourse from the comfort of your chair!' is the sort of publicity this event tends to receive. Probably, *some* of the fun would be more accurate.

The idea is that you hire actual horseraces on video. Then, in as close to racecourse atmosphere as can be achieved, those taking part are able to place bets on the races, see the video, and win or very likely lose. One disadvantage is that it is not generally possible to know any previous form for the horses, so the bets are no more than guesswork and hunches with skill at a minimum.

Even so, a lively, entertaining evening is more or less guaranteed. Details of how to find out more about this event can be found in Section 6: *Useful Addresses*.

Cost: High
Organisation: Moderate
Profit: High

Date tried	
Target profit	£
Profit (actual)	£

Very successful   worthwhile   unsuccessful

Notes/Comments

COMPUTER HIRE

The very fact that the term 'computer junkie' exists at all indicates the immense appeal computers now have for so many. This event simply makes micros available for hire.

Obviously a good range of machines and a variety of software will be needed. Borrow it all for maximum profit! People then book short amounts of time with the equipment, one or two being available for serious purposes, the majority for playing games. A running total of leading high scores will add to the interest.

Try to obtain on loan or hire an example of the very latest generation of micros for anyone who would like to see one put through its paces or try it out themselves. This activity can feature as part of a larger event like a fête or fair quite effectively.

Cost: Low
Organisation: Moderate
Profit: Low

Date tried	
Target profit	£
Profit (actual)	£

Very successful   worthwhile   unsuccessful

Notes/Comments

COOKERY BOOK

If you are of the school of thought that prefers to give people something for their money – and ideally something both useful and of good value – this could be the answer. Ask everyone you meet for a favourite recipe or two. Collect them into a booklet, garnish with decoration and illustration, pop into a moderate photocopier until done and the recipe book is ready for sale.

The value, of course, is in the quality of the recipes, so even a fairly homespun booklet can gain word-of-mouth reputation and sell in good quantity. It is very important, though, to check the recipes before including them in the booklet or you must make it very clear that you have not done so.

Cost: Low
Organisation: Considerable
Profit: Moderate

Date tried

Target profit   £

Profit (actual)   £

Very successful   worthwhile   unsuccessful

Notes/Comments

COUNTRY FAIR

A fair with a country theme or flavour might be a more accurate way to describe this activity. And incidentally, why not hold one in, near or even central to a town? All you need is a good-size patch of grass – the local football club ground might be quite satisfactory.

You can combine the traditional stalls and sideshows for a fête or fair (see Section 2: *30 ideas for your fête*) with rural crafts and activities like shearing, baling and farm equipment displays. Home baking and brewing can also be featured, possibly with prizes for the best of the bunch.

Cost: High
Organisation: Considerable
Profit: Moderate

Date tried	
Target profit	£
Profit (actual)	£

Very successful   worthwhile   unsuccessful

Notes/Comments

COVENANTING

This is now quite a well-trodden path, but if carried through successfully it can bring huge rewards. There are schools, for example, that receive between £50,000 and £60,000 over a five-year period through this activity alone. The principal emotional and intellectual appeal, of course, is in handing some of your tax, not to the taxman, but to a charity or organisation of your choice.

You will save considerable sums if you can enlist onto your planning group both an accountant and a solicitor. There are very precise regulations to be observed, so you may prefer to work through a commercial company that offers this service (see Section 6: *Useful Addresses*). Expect, however, to pay them a four-figure sum for their services. It has to be conceded that this is a fundraising system likely to be really effective in the more affluent parts of the country, for you are asking each individual to contribute a sizeable sum.

Done by you:
Cost: Moderate
Organisation: Considerable
Profit: High+

Done by a company:
Cost: High+
Organisation: Moderate
Profit: High+

Date tried	
Target profit	£
Profit (actual)	£

Very successful   worthwhile   unsuccessful

Notes/Comments

CRAFT FAIR

Some people tend to feel threatened by this sort of event, falsely believing that only work of high artistic merit would be eligible. The problem is first to find these people and then to convince them that they do have something to offer.

The income is raised from two sources:

- the charges for admission, programmes, refreshments, etc.
- revenue from the sale of the items, both 100 per cent from donated goods and an agreed percentage from other items.

If you want to broaden the event further, 'Hobbies Fair' or 'Craft and Hobbies Fair' will do well for a title. This is an activity that needs ample advance planning.

Cost: Low
Organisation: Considerable
Profit: Low

Date tried	
Target profit	£
Profit (actual)	£

Very successful   worthwhile   unsuccessful

Notes/Comments

CRAZES

Yo-yos, hula-hoops, frisbees, skateboards, ghostbusters, turtles – even, it seems, as one craze takes hold the next is already on its way. For this fundraiser to work you will need to be very astute and move in early on a craze, finding the means of obtaining the items at trade, wholesale or comparable prices. You will also need a fair measure of luck. This is because there is absolutely nothing less fashionable than a craze that has just run its course and nothing less profitable than being left with a stock of several hundred hula-hoops when no-one wants to be seen anywhere near one.

Proceed with great care, therefore. Crazes can be very profitable, but success is far from guaranteed.

Cost: High
Organisation: Simple
Profit: Moderate

Date tried	
Target profit	£
Profit (actual)	£

Very successful   worthwhile   unsuccessful

Notes/Comments

CRÈCHE

You have official government backing for this one. 'Workplace nurseries' was the term used by the Chancellor of the Exchequer in his budget speech when these were first officially encouraged, but he meant much the same thing. It is a fashionable cry and there are even financial inducements to companies to set them up.

However, you do need to do it properly. Casual child-minding by amateurs is not what we are talking about (although more informal child-minding by members of your group can also be lucrative, as long as they have been approved by the local authority). You need one or more people with NNEB or similar qualifications and, obviously, suitable premises.

One other good reason for setting up a crèche, of course, is to release members of your group to work on an event. It is a strong encouragement to come along. Err on the generous side with the staffing of it and try to begin on a small scale.

Cost: Low
Organisation: Moderate
Profit: High

Date tried	
Target profit	£
Profit (actual)	£

Very successful   worthwhile   unsuccessful

Notes/Comments

DIARIES

There are one or two different ways to do this, so some early decisions will be necessary. It is quite possible to produce a fairly inexpensive, acceptable diary geared to the requirements of your clientèle by desk-top publishing methods, possibly spirally bound. However, you may feel you do not possess the design skills, or you may simply wish to purchase for re-sale at very preferential terms (see Section 6: *Useful Addresses*). With 'personal organisers' now widely regarded as slightly passé, there is good potential for this fundraiser.

Bear in mind that sales are bound to be highly seasonal and that diaries will be bought as Christmas presents by many people as early as November. Concentrate on selling in October and early November, therefore.

Cost: Moderate
Organisation: Simple
Profit: Moderate

Date tried	
Target profit	£
Profit (actual)	£

Very successful   worthwhile   unsuccessful

Notes/Comments

DICE FOR A CAR

In effect, this is an invitation simply to donate money, although the big prize of a brand-new car has been won at events before now. The idea is to throw six or seven sixes on a single throw of the dice, so the odds are immensely unfavourable. Even so, many people will take part at the required charge in the spirit of 'you-just-never-know' illogical optimism.

Instead of a car, you could try a yacht, caravan or major holiday abroad for a family. Scrutineers, the style of throwing, the 'playing area', the backboard, etc. are all laid down very precisely. Full details of the company that provides the insurance cover against the prize being won – even additional cover in case it is won very early on in the event, in which case a *second* vehicle can be put on offer! – are in Section 6: *Useful Addresses*.

This can make a useful sum in profit, but only at a large, well-attended event and, ideally, with the big prize heavily sponsored to cover the bulk of the insurance payment (likely to be a three-figure sum). A 'hard luck' prize for the nearest loser, possibly in the form of a miniature replica of the car, is quite a good idea.

Cost: High
Organisation: Moderate
Profit: Moderate

Date tried	
Target profit	£
Profit (actual)	£

Very successful   worthwhile   unsuccessful

Notes/Comments

DINNER DANCE

To make it special for people, go for an event that is formal, up-market (even 'exclusive' perhaps?) and expensive. Don't stint, therefore, on the quality of the venue, the food, the wine or the music. You may wish to consider adding the ingredient of a first-class speaker to speak – fairly briefly! – between the dinner part and the onset of the dancing.

If you have judged your clientèle correctly and this venture is a success, consider making it an annual event.

Cost: High
Organisation: Considerable
Profit: High

Date tried	
Target profit	£
Profit (actual)	£

Very successful   worthwhile   unsuccessful

Notes/Comments

DISCOS

The area in which you operate is the vital factor here. If you are in competition with several other discos held regularly within a few miles, you would do well to turn over the page and consider the next idea. In some rural areas you might be able to create the social highlight of the week for the younger generation: try to ensure, though, that you do not become a nuisance to those not in that category.

Check with the customers carefully. There is often one disco operator whom everyone agrees provides the best show. Given the age group likely to be involved, you are strongly recommended to try keeping the bar non-alcoholic. If you do serve alcohol, it is just not worth risking prosecution by blithely serving everyone. Local youth-workers will advise you if approached for help. Be prepared also for the possibility of drug use: it is well worth consulting the local police about this in advance of the event. It may be useful to organise the whole thing in conjunction with a local youth club, since they will then advertise it for you.

Cost: High
Organisation: Considerable
Profit: High

Date tried	
Target profit	£
Profit (actual)	£

Very successful   worthwhile   unsuccessful

Notes/Comments

DONKEY DERBY

A donkey derby calls for considerable planning and preparation, so you should seriously consider using a commercial company to set it all up for you. It can be a great deal of fun, but check that you have totally adequate insurance to cover against all eventualities. It may not seem far to fall when you come off the top of a donkey – indeed, it *isn't* very far – but you would still have a problem if a nastily broken arm is the result.

Apart from fundraising through an admission charge and refreshments, you can increase the profits if local firms can be persuaded to sponsor each of the races – 'The Village Dairies Stakes', and so on. The takings will soar further if you operate a tote, but do not look to do this yourself. A local betting shop may well be prepared to give assistance.

Cost: Moderate
Organisation: Considerable
Profit: Moderate

Date tried

Target profit   £

Profit (actual)   £

Very successful   worthwhile   unsuccessful

Notes/Comments

DUTCH AUCTION

Although most people know how a Dutch auction works (if you don't, your blushes are spared by an explanation in a moment), make sure that your advance publicity explains it. They are fairly uncommon, so your event will have good novelty value.

A Dutch auction provides a rather different sort of tension from a traditional 'highest-bidder-takes-the-lot' auction. In this kind of an auction it is especially important that the auctioneer should be a professional. He or she starts at an unrealistically high figure and gradually reduces the asking price until someone cracks under the strain and clinches the deal.

One advantage of this system is that if you have large numbers of lots and a limited amount of time it can be made to work faster than the traditional-style auction where numerous bids may be made before any one item is sold. You may even wish to run an event which combines the two different formats.

Cost: Low
Organisation: Considerable
Profit: High

Date tried	
Target profit	£
Profit (actual)	£

Very successful   worthwhile   unsuccessful

Notes/Comments

FANCY DRESS

Although this can be an event in itself, namely a fancy dress competition, it will often work well as an adjunct to another function (e.g. a disco). Consider some of the other recommended activities in this book with fancy dress in mind.

It is quite a good idea to collect together a quantity of colourful and bizarre items of clothing to help out those in difficulties. They can be obtained for no more than a few pence at local jumble sales since they are exactly the sort of atrocious clothes that will not sell for any other purpose.

Try to avoid the more tired and tried themes like 'vicars and tarts'. Photographs of the event can be useful for future publicity or merely displaying on the club or committee notice-board. One thing is guaranteed: fancy dress will break down the barriers of stuffiness and awkwardness like nothing else!

Cost: Low
Organisation: Moderate
Profit: Low

Date tried

Target profit   £

Profit (actual)   £

Very successful   worthwhile   unsuccessful

Notes/Comments

FASHION SHOW

Those of us who don't attend such events sometimes find it hard to fathom the appeal that they hold, but beyond doubt they are extremely popular, even in some cases both up-market and elegant, with admission prices to match. Try to determine well in advance just how sophisticated an evening you are hoping to create.

If you can, forge a link with a local clothes store that will give sponsorship and other support. It is a good idea also to encourage a 'home designed and manufactured' garments section, perhaps offering a prize for the item judged to be the best of these.

Another possibility is to incorporate a make-up demonstration in the event. Once again, a link with a local shop may be feasible.

Cost: Moderate
Organisation: Considerable
Profit: Moderate

Date tried	
Target profit	£
Profit (actual)	£

Very successful   worthwhile   **unsuccessful**

Notes/Comments

FILL THE TUBE!

This is an extremely simple idea, but nevertheless it is a painless and steady way of collecting money over a period of time, particularly by children. Each person is asked to take a 'Smarties' or similar sweets container (preferably decorated first by covering with coloured, shiny paper) and gradually fill it with small change. This is never likely to raise a huge total, but each container will produce a deceptively large amount.

Cost: Low
Organisation: Simple
Profit: Low

Date tried	
Target profit	£
Profit (actual)	£

Very successful   worthwhile   unsuccessful

Notes/Comments

FILM CLUB

In many parts of the country access to a good film is now quite restricted. For example, Winchester recently lost its one and only cinema. Obviously, video hire has tended to take over to some extent, but there do still remain plenty of people who prefer to go out to see a film in the company of others.

Try to create a genuine feeling of a club. Occasional expert introductions, the chance for discussion after the film over a cup of coffee, help with home-movie making – all of these can add to the appeal. This type of event is not certain to make a profit, though, so gauge your audiences well. If your potential customers regard 'Carry On' films as the ultimate visual experience, they simply will not come along to see that experimental avant-garde movie shot with a hand-held camera in the central Amazonian jungle, or if they do they will not return the following week. Look to play safe until the club is fairly well established and do respond to the members' own suggestions.

Cost: Moderate
Organisation: Moderate
Profit: Low

Date tried	
Target profit	£
Profit (actual)	£

Very successful   worthwhile   unsuccessful

Notes/Comments

FIREWORKS SHOW

You can now take advantage of the fact that many people have given up having their own back-garden fireworks events. After all, at £2 per rocket can they be blamed?

Sell tickets in advance and offer a reserve date in case the weather is poor. Because so much of your show is likely to be visible from some distance, make sure that you add other ingredients to the event, like barbecued food, a beer tent and possibly music, to encourage people to pay the entry fee.

Naturally safety must be paramount. Allow only an agreed team of experienced people to set off the fireworks and use ropes to prevent spectators from coming too close. Double-check that you could not be considered in any way negligent and that your insurance cover is entirely adequate!

Cost: High
Organisation: Moderate
Profit: Moderate

Date tried	
Target profit	£
Profit (actual)	£

Very successful   worthwhile   unsuccessful

Notes/Comments

'FOR SALE' BOARDS

These can often be seen in local supermarkets and they, in fact, represent the main opposition, since they can generally be used without charge. Even so, many people will happily pay a regular sum each week for you to display their advertisement, especially if your display is in a prominent site. Therefore, if your board has a capacity of, say, 50 or 60 cards, you have a very satisfactory – and regular – source of income. So it really is true that previously empty pieces of wall-space can quite quickly be turned into a profitable fundraising idea.

Cost: Low
Organisation: Simple
Profit: Moderate

Date tried	
Target profit	£
Profit (actual)	£

Very successful   worthwhile   unsuccessful

Notes/Comments

FORTUNE TELLING

This activity could be one sideshow at a larger event or, if you find you have a talented crystal-ball gazer, reader of tea leaves and so on, it could become a regular feature at different events arranged by your group. Take care, however, that it does not drift into the rather more controversial aspects of the occult. It is quite possible to set up a light-hearted, enjoyable activity without risking causing upset through, for example, use of a ouija board or Tarot cards.

Your fortune-teller and his or her stall should become a colourful feature, just as a visiting Santa Claus adds colour – and, for the tinies, great delight – to an event around Christmas time. Such activities tend not to raise huge sums, but they do contribute usefully to the general atmosphere.

Cost: Initially high, thereafter low
Organisation: Moderate
Profit: Moderate

Date tried	
Target profit	£
Profit (actual)	£

Very successful   worthwhile   unsuccessful

Notes/Comments

GAMES EVENING

This quite simple idea can easily produce a hectic, enjoyable and financially profitable evening. A hall or large room is needed. You must find at least a dozen indoor games and arrange them around the room with one member of your group in charge of each (so it is labour intensive). Examples of suitable games are: darts, table skittles, miniature putting, nine-pin bowling, word-making games and number puzzles. Some children's board games also make very satisfactory material for this sort of event.

Each participant receives a card on arrival and has a set amount of time – 1 to 1.5 hours is ideal – to score as highly as possible. Once all the games have been tried extra attempts may be made to improve scores. At the end prizes are awarded to those with the highest scores. Take care, though, to devise a scoring system that is similar for all the games (e.g. a total of ten points maximum per game).

The games evening is an excellent way of mixing people, since you have no choice but to get involved. Whole families can take part, but consider one or two games marked 'children only'. You will not raise enormous sums in profit, but a convivial evening is more or less guaranteed.

Cost: Low
Organisation: Moderate
Profit: Low

Date tried

Target profit   £

Profit (actual)   £

Very successful   worthwhile   unsuccessful

Notes/Comments

'GREEN FINGERS GROUP'

Even more than green fingers, what this activity requires is a party of willing souls who are prepared to carry out those tasks in the garden like the weeding, the mowing, the hedge- and edge-trimming that many gardeners would prefer to forget. You need to work out a set scale of charges for the various services that you provide. Your main cost will consist of the tools required for the work. If you are able to take along with you a compost-making shredder, you may be of even greater interest to customers.

If you are giving effective publicity to your group, you may be able to obtain sponsorship from a local garden centre. It will also add enormously to the prestige of the group if you can incorporate the expertise of someone who can act as a consultant to help local gardeners tackle their problems – a sort of 'Gardeners Question Time' on legs.

Cost: Moderate – high
Organisation: Moderate
Profit: Moderate

Date tried	
Target profit	£
Profit (actual)	£

Very successful   worthwhile   unsuccessful

Notes/Comments

HOBBIES DAY/HOBBIES FAIR

Astronomers, flower arrangers, radio hams, potters, canoeists and chess-players – the sheer diversity of hobbies possible in this event makes it a thoroughly pleasing experience. Once you begin to make it known to people that a Hobbies Day is being arranged, you will be astonished at the number and variety of interests you discover, even in people you thought you knew well.

Allocate a display area to each participant and include special timed displays as appropriate. In the main, though, just allow people to browse. You can charge an admission fee, make some profits from refreshments and possibly hold a raffle, so some reasonable profits can be made on the day. Above all else, though, it will provide a fascinating day out and the chance to introduce young children to new interests, so do not allow the fundraising side to dominate. You will have succeeded if at the end people are saying 'we must hold another one sometime' – and they well might!

Cost: Low
Organisation: Considerable
Profit: Low

Date tried	
Target profit	£
Profit (actual)	£

Very successful   worthwhile   unsuccessful

Notes/Comments

HOLIDAY CHANGE

Warwick's First Law of Going on Holiday Abroad states that the last half-dozen people you meet before leaving for home all pass you a fistful of loose change. And of course it becomes totally deadweight once you set foot on home soil. It is about as much use as those plane and ferry embarkation cards that nobody ever bothers to ask you for.

If you can devise a suitable system to collect it, that 'worthless money' can become worth plenty to you. Best of all is to seek official permission to collect at an airport, ferry port or major railway terminus. Give some thought to how you will exchange it once you have a useful sum. Banks and travel agencies are unlikely to want to know unless it folds.

Cost: Low
Organisation: Simple
Profit: Low

Date tried	
Target profit	£
Profit (actual)	£

Very successful   worthwhile   unsuccessful

Notes/Comments

HOUSEHOLD CHORES

It is, of course, because these tasks are so widely disliked that there is money to be made from offering such a service. Each participant should be issued with a statement that this is a bona fide activity run by your organisation and it is also helpful to be able to show a list of the specific tasks on offer. Try to ensure that a realistic scale of charges is agreed, since jobs like car cleaning, lawn mowing, brass polishing and window cleaning are worth at least £1 if done well. Advertise your services in the local press and try to leave doorbell ringing to 'bob-a-job' teams.

Take care to encourage work of a good standard. Complaints about scratched cars and prize specimens pulled up as weeds can quite spoil the event. If many people are involved in the same geographical area, some sort of sticker or ticket to indicate 'job done' can avoid harassment.

Cost: Low
Organisation: Moderate
Profit: Moderate

Date tried	
Target profit	£
Profit (actual)	£

Very successful   worthwhile   unsuccessful

Notes/Comments

HOUSE NAMES AND NUMBERS

It is surely an undeniable fact that frequently in Britain house names and numbers cannot be read from the road. As a result, finding a house in an area you don't know can be rather taxing. This scheme would enable you to play a small part in solving the problem. Use the local press to advertise your scheme, although handbills and word -of-mouth publicity will also work well.

Hand-painted to order on attractive wood, these can justifiably be priced at £10 at least, even though your cost of materials is minimal. The project does need some publicity. Emphasise the fact that if you try to purchase this sort of item in the shops you will experience some difficulty. Your group can usefully fill this gap.

Cost: Low
Organisation: Moderate
Profit: Moderate

Date tried	
Target profit	£
Profit (actual)	£

Very successful   worthwhile   unsuccessful

Notes/Comments

HUNDRED CLUB

Or 200 Club, or 500, or perhaps just the fifty. What you need is a specific round-figure total of people who are prepared to write a standing order to participate in a series of draws. The main appeal lies in the fact that, with only a limited number involved, the odds against winning do not read like a telephone number.

You must by law return a minimum of 50 per cent of the takings in prizes, but exactly how you divide up the prize money is up to you. It is worth offering one really sizeable and attractive prize (drawn at the end of the series, ideally), together with a good number of smaller ones. For example, if every six months fifty people are paying in £20 each and you decide to return £525 in prizes, the distribution could be rather like this:

JANUARY: £50, £30, £10   FEBRUARY: £30   MARCH: £30
APRIL: £75, £20   MAY: £30   JUNE: £200, £30, £20

As people will tend to allow their standing orders to continue, it is clear that after the initial spadework a steady profit of close to £1000 per annum is possible through the above arrangement. An additional selling point, of course, is that you *could* win more than once!

Cost: Low
Organisation: Considerable
Profit: High

Date tried	
Target profit	£
Profit (actual)	£

Very successful   worthwhile   unsuccessful

Notes/Comments

ICE CREAMS, YOGURTS AND MILK SHAKES _____

You are possibly able to make delicious varieties of all three of these in the comfort of your own home. Your home-made ice cream may be acclaimed in the village, your yogurts the talk of the town. Even so, because of the ever-tightening food hygiene regulations and the dire consequences if your old and trusted recipe happened on just one occasion to offer salmonella or botulism as an added secret ingredient, you are strongly advised not to sell much home-made produce.

Instead, it is possible to buy all of the above and other similar foodstuffs at worthwhile bulk-buy prices and, since food profit margins have become so high in Britain, re-sell to good effect. An example of a firm that offers supplies and this service is listed in Section 6: *Useful Addresses*.

Cost: High
Organisation: Simple
Profit: Moderate

Date tried	
Target profit	£
Profit (actual)	£

Very successful   worthwhile   unsuccessful

Notes/Comments

'IT'S A KNOCKOUT'

In fact, it is or isn't depending on your point of view. Known to the linguistically gifted as 'Jeux sans Frontières', this is the television-inspired game that requires contestants to compete in light-hearted tests of, generally, physical skill.

The golden rule is that the sillier the competition the more laughs (in theory) are generated. Sliding down a greasy ramp dressed as a pineapple, while not appealing to this author's sense of fun, is the sort of activity that has held millions of television viewers in thrall for several years.

The cost of setting up such an event has to be high, so it can only be tried as a mass audience occasion. Health and Safety factors need to be uppermost in the minds of the planning group throughout. If gases, glues or chemicals are to be used in any games, the Control of Substances Hazardous to Health (COSHH) regulations will apply. Your local Citizen's Advice Bureau should be able to help in connection with this. If you can get local firms to enter teams, they can often be persuaded to give support, make their own costumes and so on. The nature of the event alone allows for some quite zany local publicity, such as that human pineapple handing out advertising leaflets in the shopping precinct.

Cost: High
Organisation: Considerable
Profit: Moderate

Date tried	
Target profit	£
Profit (actual)	£

Very successful   worthwhile   unsuccessful

Notes/Comments

JAIL-BREAK

This fairly unusual event will ideally start from a real prison. Otherwise use a fictitious one set up specifically for the occasion. Each participant (or team) is set the challenge of travelling as far away from the prison as possible within 24 hours. Any form of transport may be used, but none is provided. Either no money at all or very little is made available to those taking part. You may wish to allow a small range of standard items for survival, such as a pack of sandwiches and a map.

Income can be generated in two ways. Inevitably there is sponsorship of the brave souls prepared to take up this challenge, or you could set up a competition whereby people are asked to estimate how far or where the winning team will get to in the time available. It is an activity that has considerable potential for media publicity, but try to time it to avoid a period of prison riots or roof-top protests!

Cost: Low
Organisation: Moderate
Profit: High

Date tried	
Target profit	£
Profit (actual)	£

Very successful   worthwhile   unsuccessful

Notes/Comments

JOINING FORCES

Imagine that a very major event – a country fair, say, or an open-air pop concert – is taking place somewhere in your area. You contact the organisers and offer to promote their event at the gate through selling stickers, flyers or whatever else is agreed between you. A simple 'I was at . . . ' or ' I ♥   . . ' may be as satisfactory as anything else. You then take, ideally, the revenue from what you manage to sell, or at least a healthy percentage.

The extent of your success will hinge to a considerable extent on the nature, the scale and the success of the event on which you hitch a lift. It is admittedly a shade parasitic, but if you actually add to what the organisers have been able to set up, you may contribute to the occasion. It can be highly lucrative, but you will need to move exceptionally quickly and efficiently early on in your planning.

Cost: Moderate
Organisation: Moderate
Profit: High

Date tried	
Target profit	£
Profit (actual)	£

Very successful   worthwhile   unsuccessful

Notes/Comments

JOKE BOOKS

As with quiz books, with this idea there is the great advantage that people actually receive something for their money. Ask a group of friends (and their other friends) to provide their favourite jokes, and approach some well-known people who do not mind the publicity, e.g. the 'Mayor's favourite joke'. Make sure that not all of the items you collect are hoary old has-beens of jokes and groan-producing one-liners. Best of all, use little sketches and cartoons to add the effect.

Even a fairly homespun collection with photocopied sheets can be sold for 40p or 50p. It is most important, though, to leave out absolutely everything that could cause offence to even the most sensitive of readers. 'If in doubt, leave it out' should be the editor's motto, so leave out racist and sexist jokes, any with offensive language or sexual innuendo.

Cost: Moderate
Organisation: Moderate
Profit: Moderate

Date tried	
Target profit	£
Profit (actual)	£
Very successful worthwhile unsuccessful	
Notes/Comments	

LOCAL NEWSLETTERS

How successfully you can operate this activity will depend on exactly how effective the existing local newspapers are. If they in any way fall short of people's expectations, this is worth a try. Be warned, though. It is extremely labour-intensive in that your copy will need considerable preparation and a whole production team will need to be at work to meet your publication deadlines.

You must try to gain the support of local businesses. Your revenue will come far more easily from advertising than from whatever you decide to charge per copy.

Cost: Moderate
Organisation: Considerable
Profit: Moderate

Date tried	
Target profit	£
Profit (actual)	£

Very successful   worthwhile   unsuccessful

Notes/Comments

MAGAZINES

You either produce your own, in which case you will need a capable and dedicated editorial team that can produce a considerable amount of good-quality copy, or you could make use of a specialist firm (for this, see Section 6: *Useful Addresses*). As an effective fundraising idea a one-off publication designed to celebrate an anniversary or specific achievement has far more potential than a regularly-appearing magazine.

This idea is not one that falls into the sure-fire success category. Considerable planning and a little luck are needed! Try to check in advance the interest level of the likely customers.

(See also YEAR BOOK)

If you do it yourself
Cost: High
Organisation: Considerable
Profit: Moderate

If you employ others
Cost: Low
Organisation: Moderate
Profit: Low

Date tried	
Target profit	£
Profit (actual)	£

Very successful   worthwhile   unsuccessful

Notes/Comments

MOBILE SUPPER

This is now quite an established event, but it is a useful fundraiser and does provide a sociable time for all concerned. It requires a group of people each of whom is prepared to provide (without charge!) one course of a meal for a group of visitors. The visitors themselves must be prepared to pay generously for the opportunity to dine out at a variety of venues.

The detailed organisation of this needs to be precise. See that everyone receives a map or sketch-map, a time schedule and further instructions, names of the volunteer hosts and hostesses and so on. It is essential that you don't end up with numerous hungry people driving round the area lost and a selection of delicious meals going lukewarm! Naturally, a sensible policy regarding alcohol is most important.

Cost: Low
Organisation: Moderate
Profit: Moderate

Date tried	
Target profit	£
Profit (actual)	£

Very successful   **worthwhile**   **unsuccessful**

Notes/Comments

MODEL TRAINS

This is really not much more than a fête sideshow that can be developed further if you judge the interest is there locally. The train or trains run on a track that is marked out in sections or with town names. When the whole track has been backed by the participants the train is set running, the winner being decided by where it stops. A clockwork train will run down naturally, of course, but if you use an electrically powered layout have someone behind a screen gradually slow and then stop the train. You will find the amount of tension and excitement created quite surprising! The size of the stakes and the prizes can be varied to add to the interest.

A competition like this can be incorporated into a larger event like a model trains exhibition quite effectively.

Cost: Low
Organisation: Simple
Profit: Low

Date tried	
Target profit	£
Profit (actual)	£

Very successful   worthwhile   unsuccessful

Notes/Comments

MUGS

This has nothing to do with the attitude of the more ruthless fundraising team towards the customers. It involves the bulk-buying and possible overprinting of ordinary drinking mugs for re-sale.

It is an activity that does not require too much comment, for it is more or less self-explanatory. If you have the mugs overprinted with the crest, logo or name of your organisation it will naturally bring some publicity, but will not necessarily increase the potential sales figure. The project is unlikely to raise huge sums, but is still worth trying if you can to obtain a good quality product (see Section 6: *Useful Addresses*).

Cost: Moderate
Organisation: Moderate
Profit: Low

Date tried

Target profit   £

Profit (actual)   £

Very successful   **worthwhile**   **unsuccessful**

Notes/Comments

NAMETAPES

Mainly for schools
This will inevitably work best if the school policy is that nametapes are obligatory on children's clothes! Whether or not this is the case, a helpful service is provided and the company will generally give a set sum of money for each order received. You simply need to compile a sufficiently large order for a reasonable sum to be raised. This is unlikely to become a major fundraiser, partly because the tapes will usually come in sufficiently large quantities to see the children well into middle-age.

See Section 6: *Useful Addresses.*

Cost: Low
Organisation: Moderate
Profit: Low

Date tried	
Target profit	£
Profit (actual)	£

Very successful   worthwhile   unsuccessful

Notes/Comments

NON-EVENT

This sounds to be just what every fundraiser most wants to avoid. The basic idea, though, is that your potential supporters are asked to send a cheque in return for *not* being asked to buy tickets, help set up an event, give up precious time to attend and so on. If the organisation can undertake not to look for further support for a while after the 'non-event', so much the better. It may sound rather daft but it can work well.

The key to success lies in the effective wording of the literature you send out to potential cheque-writers. As an idea it still has a reasonably high element of novelty to it.

Cost: Low
Organisation: Simple
Profit: Moderate

Date tried	
Target profit	£
Profit (actual)	£

Very successful   worthwhile   unsuccessful

Notes/Comments

NON-UNIFORM DAY

Mainly for schools

Sometimes known as 'wear what you like' days (perhaps rather unwisely) these are enjoyable occasions for those taking part and also have the advantage that they are extremely easy to organise. Periodically (and not too often, it is recommended) pupils are allowed to wear casual clothing, as long as it is not too extreme, instead of the official school uniform – on payment of a small fee. Remarkable though it may seem, most children will willingly provide 25p or so for this privilege.

Support is sometimes increased if the money raised is to be equally divided between school funds and a charity. A proof-of-payment card could be issued to each participant so that, if challenged, it can be produced. A fine for non-production can be considered.

Even larger sums can be raised if the rule is not payment of a sum of money, but instead things like bottles of drink or craft items are brought in. Suddenly you have dozens, or even hundreds, of bottles for that bottle stall at the fête. Organisations other than schools can join in this kind of event if fancy dress is worn in, for example, a bank for charity fundraising.

Cost: Low
Organisation: Simple
Profit: Moderate

Date tried	
Target profit	£
Profit (actual)	£

Very successful   worthwhile   unsuccessful

Notes/Comments

PARABLE OF THE TALENTS

This has only a limited amount to do with what goes on in Matthew Chapter 25. The idea is that each participant receives the same sum of money (£1? £5?) to start them off and must then use skill and ingenuity to increase this amount as much as possible within a set period of time. Six months or one year are suitable time spans.

At the very least, even if the money has been lost on a faller in the 3.30 at Aintree, the original sum must be returned when the event finishes. Careful nurturing of the money, possibly by using some of the ideas suggested in this book, should ensure that the total given out is multiplied many times over. An occasional newsletter can stimulate greater interest (or competition, if a prize is on offer for the highest sum raised) and can also be used to spread ideas about how the sum could be increased further.

Cost: High
Organisation: Moderate
Profit: High

Date tried

Target profit   £

Profit (actual)   £

Very successful   worthwhile   unsuccessful

Notes/Comments

PAVEMENT ARTISTS

For those who prefer their fundraising in the more traditional style, this is an idea worth considering. Unless the pitches to be used are on your own patch, you will need local authority permission to create your masterpieces on the public pavements. Obviously, a sheltered shopping precinct will be ideal.

You can either make this a free-for-all (but with a set charge per pitch!), all-join-in mass activity or you may prefer to offer higher quality exhibits from the more talented artists that you can find. Don't forget to put a few coins in the hat(s) to encourage the donors!

Cost: Low
Organisation: Simple
Profit: Low

Date tried	
Target profit	£
Profit (actual)	£

Very successful   worthwhile   unsuccessful

Notes/Comments

PET SHOW/FLOWER SHOW _____

These would normally be run as separate events, of course, but you may wish to consider a joint 'Pet and Flower Show'. Amateurs who would never normally display their animals or flowers need to be convinced that the family mongrel or fairly ordinary pot-plants are actually worthy of inclusion in this event. The best advice, therefore, is to aim for something not too exclusive and to play down the element of competition. An attractive venue obviously helps, but it must have good access for the delivery of all the prize specimens.

Funds are raised mainly by the entrance fee. If you are considering using a celebrity to act as judge, try, for example, for a local dog-owner who has achieved success at Cruft's.

Cost: Low
Organisation: Considerable
Profit: Low

Date tried	
Target profit	£
Profit (actual)	£

Very successful   worthwhile   unsuccessful

Notes/Comments

PETTICOAT LANE

This project is similar to a sale of goods or a craft fair, but there is an essential difference in that when setting up a 'Petticoat Lane' market you strive to create an authentic market atmosphere. The traders can be encouraged to dress up, work on their sales patter and market cries and so on. It is an event that will work almost as well indoors as in the open air.

The traders can be charged roughly £5 per pitch. Make sure, also, that members of your group run one or two stalls to swell the profits. Check carefully on food hygiene regulations – for example , regarding the wrapping of cakes and biscuits – if food sales are involved. If you can manage to borrow or construct at least one genuine-looking market stall, it can add greatly to the atmosphere, even if others are trading off tables or out of suitcases.

Cost: Low
Organisation: Moderate
Profit: Moderate

Date tried	
Target profit	£
Profit (actual)	£

Very successful   worthwhile   unsuccessful

Notes/Comments

PHOTOGRAPHS

When that cellophane-wrapped pack of school photographs of your child is hauled out of the school bag a few weeks before Christmas, the asking price will be at least £4 or £5. Set against this the cost of enlarging a standard colour print at around £1.50 and it is clear that you should be able to undercut the professionals with a respectable profit margin in hand.

Keep to a set range of picture sizes and concentrate on portraits, especially of people's children. Above all else, do not assume that most members of your organisation should be able to do the photography work. Perhaps they could, but the truth is that the vast majority can't.

Cost: Moderate
Organisation: Moderate
Profit: Moderate

Date tried	
Target profit	£
Profit (actual)	£
Very successful	worthwhile unsuccessful
Notes/Comments	

PLANT SALE

The trickiest part in preparing for this activity tends to be assembling your team of contributors. However, once you have a good number of volunteers prepared to grow cuttings, flowers from seed, herbs and small shrubs, you will find you soon have a good stock of items for only a minimal outlay. Another approach to consider is allowing others to sell their plants at your stall(s) in return for a donation to the funds.

It will help considerably if you can compile your own catalogue and circulate it. Check the prices at local garden centres, who are, after all, your main opposition and try to operate at markedly lower prices, in part because some of your stock will inevitably be less hardy than theirs.

For further similar ideas, see GREEN FINGERS GROUP.

Cost: Moderate
Organisation: Considerable
Profit: Moderate

Date tried	
Target profit	£
Profit (actual)	£

Very successful   worthwhile   unsuccessful

Notes/Comments

PLAYS AND CONCERTS

Amateurs are sometimes too modest about their shows and concerts. There are appalling exceptions, of course, but most amateur shows are worth at least £2 per ticket. A simple tip, though, is to leave the final decision on charges until the last feasible moment. Base the price on the evidence of the rehearsals. Don't over-price it, but bear in mind that people actually become suspicious of what is exceptionally cheap.

Make sure you add to the total profit through programme sales and refreshments. Consider, too, the idea of taping the performance. (See TAPE THE SHOW.)

Cost: High
Organisation: Considerable
Profit: Moderate

Date tried	
Target profit	£
Profit (actual)	£

Very successful   worthwhile   unsuccessful

Notes/Comments

POSTAGE STAMPS

Ask everyone you can find to save their stamps for you. They can all be used in bulk to raise cash, but a more original – and potentially more lucrative – approach is to sift out the 10 to 20 per cent that are more unusual and would be of interest to collectors.

Take the trouble to find out how to handle stamps correctly (the Stanley Gibbons organisation have a very helpful publication). You can present the stamps either in packets or individually on strips or in small booklets. If you can, find a local philatelist who can value the stamps appropriately.

This activity is extremely fiddly and quite time-consuming also, but it does have good potential for the raising of funds.

Cost: Low
Organisation: Considerable
Profit: Moderate

Date tried	
Target profit	£
Profit (actual)	£

Very successful   worthwhile   unsuccessful

Notes/Comments

POSTER CLUB

From Winnie-the-Pooh and Postman Pat on the nursery wall, through pouting rock-bands and 'Save the Whale' posters on teenage walls to the high-quality art reproductions that Mum and Dad may purchase, there is an immense market for posters and a poster club can be the answer. It can be set up through bulk purchases – with bulk-order size discounts – from local shops or through an organisation that aims to help establish such a club (see Section 6: *Useful Addresses*).

Keeping up the momentum and communicating satisfactorily with the club members are the two biggest challenges. You will need also to send precise orders or, ideally, reach a sale-or-return agreement with your supplier.

Cost: Low
Organisation: Moderate
Profit: Moderate

Date tried	
Target profit	£
Profit (actual)	£

Very successful   worthwhile   unsuccessful

Notes/Comments

POT POURRI

You will probably need to do some background reading on the subject first (see the book titles below). You then collect the ingredients – and they do of course come free of charge in the hedgerows, spread the word and you are in business. The simplest form of packaging involves no more than muslin and ribbon, but you may wish to buy plastic boxes or even small pottery containers.

This sort of item is generally popular and can be sold at craft fairs, bazaars, etc., as well as by mail order.

Books on the subject:
Potpourri – a practical guide by Mary Lane (Bishopgate Press)
Incense and other fragrant concoctions by Ann Tucker Fettner (Hutchinson)
Potpourri and other fragrant delights by Jacqueline Heriteau (Penguin)
The book of pot pourri by Penny Black (published in association with the National Trust)

Cost: Low
Organisation: Simple
Profit: Low

Date tried	
Target profit	£
Profit (actual)	£

Very successful   worthwhile   unsuccessful

Notes/Comments

QUILTS AND SIMILAR STITCHING

A cast-of-thousands quilt can be extremely effective. First find your willing volunteers, then make them aware of the precise dimensions of the quilt sections that are required. Supply materials where required and find somebody competent to put the whole thing together.

Consider also the possibility of making for sale some or all of the following:

tea cosies   bags   changing mats   napkins

Another idea worth considering if you hold regular events to raise funds is purchasing a long roll of gingham material, then cutting and hemming the edges to create a set of ten or a dozen tablecloths. You will not actually be raising funds through doing this, but they will add colour and attractiveness to a whole host of other occasions and make for more successful fundraising in the future.

Cost: Moderate
Organisation: Considerable
Profit: Moderate

Date tried

Target profit   £

Profit (actual)   £

Very successful   worthwhile   unsuccessful

Notes/Comments

QUIZ BOOKLETS

A booklet of approximately 100 general knowledge questions will appeal to all quiz devotees. Each booklet need only cost a few pence to produce, but can be sold for at least 30p. If you plan to sell 1000 or more, advertisers will be quite interested in giving support. The time-scale needs to allow for the quite elaborate business of distributing and selling: plan at least two months for this.

This venture works far better if prizes are on offer for the best set of answers received by a closing date. One important tip, though: avoid the most thumbed and remembered trivia games quiz books when compiling your questions. The setting of the questions can be extremely time-consuming, so if each member of the committee collects ten each considerable time can be saved.

Cost: High
Organisation: Considerable
Profit: Moderate

Date tried

Target profit   £

Profit (actual)   £

Very successful   worthwhile   unsuccessful

Notes/Comments

QUIZ SUPPER

Everyone pays a set amount which covers the meal, wine and the quiz. Questions are answered by the whole table, so no-one is left feeling too ignorant. It helps to have a short simple quiz on the table as people arrive. The main quiz works well with 5 or 6 rounds before supper, then 4 or 5 afterwards. All results are announced at the end (running scores kept on a board adds to the tension) and the winners receive small prizes. Six people to each table works well, as does encouraging the donation of the food and not having a booby prize! With 90–100 participants, a net profit of £250 to £300 is perfectly possible, especially if a raffle forms part of the evening. The quiz can be even greater fun if a joker card can be played on one chosen round with the team's score for that round doubled.

This is a thoroughly good event – both a thoroughly entertaining evening for all participants and a highly satisfactory 'little earner'.

Cost: High
Organisation: Considerable
Profit: Moderate

Date tried	
Target profit	£
Profit (actual)	£

Very successful   worthwhile   unsuccessful

Notes/Comments

RECYCLING

What could be better than a fundraising activity that is also environmentally sound?
The item WASTE PAPER COLLECTION deals with the money-raising potential of old
newspapers and magazines, but you should also consider card, aluminium and even
plastics, as well as more or less all forms of scrap metal.

Visit your nearest rubbish collection centre and talk to the staff there. They should be
able to advise you on the best local opportunities. As long as you have a suitable storage
area and appropriate transport, this is a fundraiser with ever-growing potential.

Cost: Low
Organisation: Considerable
Profit: High

Date tried	
Target profit	£
Profit (actual)	£

Very successful   worthwhile   unsuccessful

Notes/Comments

REFRESHMENTS STALL/CAFÉ

When you consider the unlovely roadside snack bars and some of the more unappetizing and unhealthy fast foods available today, you should feel well able to provide genuine competition. Your café may, of course, be simply an adjunct to some other event and take the form of something slightly more ambitious than the coffee and biscuits that most people provide. If the café itself is the *raison d'etre*, you will need above all else a site that people actually have cause to visit or pass: it must also be situated in a legal position, parking nearby must be feasible and essential services (particularly water and electricity) must be readily to hand.

Acquaint yourself thoroughly with food and hygiene regulations. Just one example of how you could be in breach is to sell items like cakes, biscuits and buns to take away unwrapped. If you purchase your own raw materials in bulk at cash and carry prices you will find your profit margins quite considerable, so go for good quality in what you offer. Try to agree a sale or return deal if you don't fancy being left with 800 unwanted tea-bags and embarrassing quantities of sugar and flour. An hour spent checking the opposition's prices is well worthwhile!

Cost: High
Organisation: Considerable
Profit: Moderate

Date tried	
Target profit	£
Profit (actual)	£

Very successful   worthwhile   unsuccessful

Notes/Comments

RELAY MARATHON

Because most of us feel a shade reluctant at the prospect of 26 miles 385 yards (42kms), when publicising this idea the emphasis should be on the relay part of it. Teams of between 4 and 24 run the actual distance in stages, ideally around a small local route several times to enable spectators to stay in touch with the event. Just let each person run as much as he or she can manage.

The fundraising part is in running a competition to estimate the winning time or the time taken by each team. If each of the teams arranges its own little competition you will obviously be likely to make more out of it. You may want to offer a prize for the highest sum raised. Let everyone find sponsors if they really must, but these other approaches can also be very productive.

Cost: Low
Organisation: Considerable
Profit: Moderate

Date tried

Target profit   £

Profit (actual)   £

Very successful   worthwhile   unsuccessful

Notes/Comments

RETURNABLE BOTTLES

This idea has the advantage of being ecologically sound. However, you do need plenty of people who are prepared to collect and contribute the bottles. The point is that to all but the desperate 5p or 10p back on a bottle means very little: a collection of 500 such bottles, though, begins to be of interest.

For storage, empty wine cases can be useful. Many pubs and off-licences will be prepared to pass these on to you. Ensure that you have a satisfactory filing system, so that the different types of bottle are sorted as you receive them and not when you have a four-figure total. One small snag is that not every corner-shop retailer will be delighted to receive your 250 lemonade bottles when he has a queue of fifteen impatient customers right through the shop, so try to reach amicable local agreements in advance.

Cost: Low
Organisation: Considerable
Profit: Low

Date tried	
Target profit	£
Profit (actual)	£

Very successful   worthwhile   unsuccessful

Notes/Comments

RUN YOU OWN PUB!

It is a great deal easier to do this than most people imagine. However, make sure that you put in your licence application extremely early. It may seem absurd that weeks of advance notice are required, but this is the system. Also, you would be unwise to commit yourself too far before that licence is confirmed. It can be refused.

Include a good range of low-alcohol and non-alcoholic drinks. Some form of entertainment is also very desirable, possibly a folk group, a comedian or a combination of acts to provide a variety show. Creation of a good atmosphere is important, so pay some attention to lighting and décor. If you can, decorate the 'pub' to suggest a particular theme (e.g. old-time Music Hall, naval, futuristic). You may even wish to encourage the customers to attend in fancy dress.

You should find it feasible to improve quite considerably on actual pub prices and still make a useful profit.

Cost: High
Organisation: Considerable
Profit: Moderate

Date tried	
Target profit	£
Profit (actual)	£

Very successful   worthwhile   unsuccessful

Notes/Comments

SCHOOL GOAL

Mainly for schools

This is a football-based fundraising idea designed for schools and school-linked organisations. It offers a four-figure sum as the top prize and is based on the year's F.A. Cup Final. It boasts of high profit margins for participating schools and guarantees that, should there be a loss made, that sum will be refunded.

I am aware of schools that use this competition, but have no direct experience of it personally, so can neither recommend it nor warn you off. If you wish to find out more, further details can be found in Section 6: *Useful Addresses*.

Cost: Low
Organisation: Simple
Profit: Moderate

Date tried	
Target profit	£
Profit (actual)	£

Very successful   worthwhile   unsuccessful

Notes/Comments

SHOESHINE

This is of course more associated with turning an honest dime in the struggle for survival during the Depression than a potential fundraising activity in the 1990s. Even so, it is an activity that can raise a useful sum.

The site you choose is absolutely critical. It must be prominent, in a busy, crowded setting and ideally in an affluent part of town. Make it very clear that the shoe-shining is in aid of a good cause and you should find people prepared to pay 50 pence for two or three minutes of being pampered. It is an activity that will not produce a huge sum, but it should still be worth doing.

Cost: Low
Organisation: Simple
Profit: Low

Date tried	
Target profit	£
Profit (actual)	£

Very successful   worthwhile   unsuccessful

Notes/Comments

SILENT AUCTION

This can either be run as a complete event in itself or as one of the attractions at, say, a large Summer Fair or Christmas Bazaar. The various lots are arranged with a blank sheet of paper by each one. Bidders are invited to write their bids against as many lots as they wish to a clearly understood time limit (one hour or 1.5 perhaps, depending on the number of lots and the scale of the event). Note that not all the lots need be auctioned to the same time limit, especially as you will want to stagger the paperwork and general administration.

When the time is up the successful bidders are announced and the sales completed. As ever with auctions, the quality of the lots is the really critical factor. Go for good-quality items, and if necessary supplement what you can obtain through donations with a few purchased goods. Don't forget to put a reasonable reserve price on those or you might end up making a loss!

Cost: High
Organisation: Simple
Profit: High

Date tried	
Target profit	£
Profit (actual)	£

Very successful   worthwhile   unsuccessful

Notes/Comments

STICKERS _____

One little fringe benefit attached to this activity is that at least some of the stickers can promote your organisation and its work. In setting it all up, you have a simple choice to make: you either buy the stickers ready-made for re-sale or have your own designs produced. Whichever way you jump, the precise quantity to be ordered needs to be calculated extremely carefully.

As with all orders, bulk quantities are significantly more economical per item. You may therefore wish to order an extra-large number of stickers to promote the group and then use them regularly stuck onto your posters, advertising copy, tickets, etc. It helps considerably to build up an identity and 'image' for the group.

Cost: Moderate
Organisation: Moderate
Profit: Low

Date tried	
Target profit	£
Profit (actual)	£
Very successful worthwhile unsuccessful	
Notes/Comments	

STREET PARTY (AMERICAN SUPPER STYLE) ───────

You need not wait for the next royal wedding or England winning the World Cup before organising a street party. Indeed, you are strongly advised not to! Any occasion – someone's special birthday, a 'midsummer madness' party – will suffice as long as people can be inveigled to attend.

The American Supper part of it is essential if you are to turn out a useful profit. The idea is that everyone pays a ticket fee to attend the party and the food is provided by each person bringing a contribution, preferably of something home-made.

Additional entertainments are optional and may well not prove necessary if you can establish a sufficiently infectious atmosphere. Even so, it is a good idea to provide some background music, especially early on. Check with the police and local authority for permission to go ahead!

Cost: High
Organisation: Considerable
Profit: High

Date tried	
Target profit	£
Profit (actual)	£

Very successful   worthwhile   unsuccessful

Notes/Comments

STUNTS

If you are seeking publicity a well-prepared, original stunt takes some beating. Let people know well ahead of the occasion what is going to happen and if it coincides with a 'quiet news day' you may manage to attract a good deal of media coverage. Bear in mind, though, that such events have been known to go wrong before now. Check the details carefully with the local police and any other interested parties.

You may wish to run a 'stunts ideas' competition involving members of your group. Remember, you are looking for a completely crazy idea that is unusual enough to attract attention. People have already pulled 10-ton trucks in teams and lain in a bath-tub full of baked beans for a ridiculous length of time, so find something *new*. Unless what you set up is so sensational that people will be prepared to pay for admission, we are talking about sponsorship for the fundraising.

Cost: Low
Organisation: Considerable
Profit: Moderate

Date tried	
Target profit	£
Profit (actual)	£

Very successful   **worthwhile**   **unsuccessful**

Notes/Comments

SUNFLOWERGROWING

Anything growing really, but this activity is particularly dramatic with sunflowers. You supply those taking part – and children particularly love to – with the seeds and the rules, having decided first whether it is to be, yet again, a sponsored event (1p per inch or centimetre sounds very little, but can be quite lucrative for a sunflower in a good summer) or a competition to guess the height of the winning flower.

It helps greatly if you have some means like regular meetings or a newsletter to enable people to stay informed about how the event is going. Otherwise they tend to become rather isolated sunflowergrowers.

Cost: Low
Organisation: Simple
Profit: Low

Date tried	
Target profit	£
Profit (actual)	£

Very successful   worthwhile   unsuccessful

Notes/Comments

TABLE SALE (OR SUITCASE SALE OR GARAGE SALE) ‒‒‒‒‒

This activity is little more than a foul-weather version of the popular Car Boot Sale. Each participant hires a 'pitch', whether a table provided or an area on which to display the suitcase and its contents, for £4 or £5, so a profit is guaranteed as the acceptances roll in. A reduction of, say, £1 for booking in advance is generally worth offering. If the allocation of pitches is 'first-come-first-served', make this clear beforehand. Unseemly rows have been known over who is to have that very particular pitch.

These events work best when they come in a series, thereby gaining momentum and with luck a reputation that they are worth attending. Try, therefore, to have your next event pre-planned so that the date, time and venues can be advertised at the previous sale and successful participants can re-book at once. As with jumble sales, the punters tend to be far too interested in the bargains available to be terribly concerned about light refreshments, but this gesture will always be much appreciated by your stallholders – and you do want them to return next time!

Cost: Low
Organisation: Simple
Profit: Low

Date tried	
Target profit	£
Profit (actual)	£

Very successful   worthwhile   unsuccessful

Notes/Comments

TALENT SHOW

This can be immense fun and also has the potential to do wonders for everyone's morale. However, with many people, inhibitions and excessive modesty are the initial barriers to be broken down. The secret is to decide who really has a talent worthy of display in a showcase.

It is a good idea to have separate junior and senior sections. For the best performance in each category a small prize can be awarded. It is vital to check out the performances thoroughly beforehand. If you do find anyone – or any particular material – embarrassingly bad or simply in poor taste, remember it is far kinder to find yourself unable to fit him or her into the terribly crowded programme.

Cost: Moderate
Organisation: Considerable
Profit: Low

Date tried	
Target profit	£
Profit (actual)	£

Very successful   worthwhile   unsuccessful

Notes/Comments

TAPE THE SHOW!

This is really the follow-up to another event, but can be used as an additional fundraiser. If your organisation is producing a play, concert or similar event, ensure that someone makes a high-quality audio or video tape for sale as a momento.

Careful editing will be necessary, since it is remarkable how long the silences and background noise can sound in an unedited version of, for example, a carol service or a concert. The cost to you is in time, for the profit margin is quite considerable.

Cost: Moderate
Organisation: Moderate
Profit: Low

Date tried	
Target profit	£
Profit (actual)	£

Very successful   worthwhile   unsuccessful

Notes/Comments

T-SHIRTS/SWEATSHIRTS, Etc. ───────────────

There are several items of clothing that can be bought in bulk quantities and re-sold advantageously. Although T-shirts and sweatshirts are probably the most promising lines, Blagdon Cricket Club near Bristol used to sell huge quantities of ladies' tights to boost club funds. The scornful comments and the jokes ceased the moment other people realised just how profitable it was.

There is quite a competitive market, so check carefully before you stock up with shelf after shelf of possibly unappealing merchandise. If your organisation has a crest, logo or slogan, consider whether this might add to sales (it obviously narrows your potential market). It is generally possible to order a sample item and this is worth doing. The payment system often involves despatch of your cheque a week or ten days after receipt of the goods, so if cash-flow is not your greatest strength, some intensive selling will be necessary. Only obtain the extra-large size through individual orders or you will risk having to store items that are steadily gathering dust.

An added advantage of this activity, of course, is the additional sense of commitment that some may feel in wearing 'the club sweatshirt'.

Cost: Low
Organisation: Considerable
Profit: Low

Date tried	
Target profit	£
Profit (actual)	£

Very successful   worthwhile   unsuccessful

Notes/Comments

TOY MAKING

There is a host of small hand-made toys that can be sold at a good profit. Bean-bags, finger puppets, pop-up puppets, masks, mobiles, woollen balls, knitted cats, dogs, pandas and rabbits, clothes for dolls – all can be manufactured to your own design or with the aid of any one of a whole range of books that give advice on the subject.

Bear in mind that public awareness of the need for toys to be *safe* has increased greatly. Special care is needed, therefore, over the use of buttons and beads that could become dangerous, over use of sharp metal or wooden corners and potentially harmful material to stuff the toys.

Cost: Moderate
Organisation: Considerable
Profit: Low

Date tried	
Target profit	£
Profit (actual)	£

Very successful   worthwhile   unsuccessful

Notes/Comments

TRADING STAMPS/PETROL TOKENS/'FREE OFFERS', Etc. ___

It is quite hard to avoid them in everyday life, yet only a minority seek to collect and use them. Encourage all the members of your group and their friends (and theirs) to collect them and pool them. You will be pleasantly surprised at how quickly you have the means to buy goods to the value of £30, £40 or even £50.

If it really is a *free* offer, you will still need the cost of at least one stamp, possibly with post and packing costs as well. You will also, of course, need the tokens for the item. As you should have goods to the value of a few pounds, it is still worth bothering about. Don't take the trouble, though, if the item in question has the brand-name of the cereals, the jam, or whatever, on it. You simply will not be able to use it in the same way – as an auction lot, raffle prize, in a sale of goods – if its past history is obvious. One small point to bear in mind concerns the 'only one per household' rule that sometimes applies. Other members of the group will need to agree to act as recipients.

Cost: Low
Organisation: Moderate
Profit: Moderate

Date tried	
Target profit	£
Profit (actual)	£

Very successful   worthwhile   unsuccessful

Notes/Comments

VINTAGE CAR RALLY

The harsh truth is that car journeys in the 1920s and 1930s were generally cold, uncomfortable, inefficient and far slower than most people could tolerate today. Over the years, though, nostalgia has taken over and there is widespread affection for the early cars. A well-organised rally, therefore, can attract large crowds.

Start with people you know and you may be surprised at how many have a vehicle that may not be officially vintage or veteran, but is still of interest. Then contact car companies, showrooms and the experts in the field. This is the kind of activity that can attract sponsorship, so you may be able to mount quite a large-scale event. One difficulty may be finding a sufficiently large space. Charge for admission, food and drink and, if you can arrange it, for a ride on one or two of the most fascinating models.

Cost: Moderate
Organisation: Considerable
Profit: Moderate

Date tried

Target profit   £

Profit (actual)   £

Very successful   worthwhile   unsuccessful

Notes/Comments

WASHING CARS

This can raise quite good sums simply because it is a chore that so few people enjoy. However, unless done properly it can lose you a friend or two when, for example, somebody takes a Brillo pad to the bonnet to deal with the dead insects.

Consider offering a comparable service for the inside of the vehicle. 'Car valet service' is the somewhat pretentious phrase used by the companies that do this. They charge upwards of £30 for what they do, so even though you are amateurs, probably using less sophisticated equipment and possibly not achieving quite the same effect, do not underprice the service you are providing.

One small warning is necessary. A group in Hampshire set up a scheme like this in the height of the summer and because water was in short supply at the time, they received some adverse publicity for their pains. It even resulted in the water company ruling that in their view what was being done was illegal since a 'commercial operation', as they saw it, was taking place using a private dwelling water source. This was obviously an unfortunate ruling for them and indicative of the sort of snares that can surround even the most innocent-sounding fundraising activity.

Cost: Low
Organisation: Simple
Profit: Moderate

Date tried	
Target profit	£
Profit (actual)	£

Very successful   **worthwhile**   **unsuccessful**

Notes/Comments

WASTEPAPER COLLECTION

This activity concerns mainly newspapers and magazines. Bulk collection is not all that difficult when, for example, the *Sunday Times* currently produces nine or ten different sections and well over 200 pages. There are one or two small snags, however.

The first of these is the need for a large fire and vandal-proof store together with suitable insurance cover. The second problem results from the general British lethargy regarding re-cycling. Partly due to an acute lack of de-inking plants, which are vital if better quality paper is to be produced, the price rate on offer from your local paper collection company will vary hugely from around £40 per ton to as low as £5 to £10 per ton. It is an activity that you may need to halt, therefore, if the rewards fall disastrously.

Cost: Low
Organisation: Moderate
Profit: Moderate

Date tried	
Target profit	£
Profit (actual)	£

Very successful   worthwhile   unsuccessful

Notes/Comments

'WHAT'S THE TIME?' COMPETITION _____

This very simple idea does seem to have general appeal, possibly because it is not immediately apparent that your chance of winning is one in quite-a-few-thousand. At the 'launch ceremony' you wind up a clock and then seal it in a box. (It's not a bad idea if the clock can be heard ticking away from inside the box.) The challenge is to estimate to the last second how many days, hours, minutes and seconds it will run before stopping.

It is worth providing some specifications regarding the clock if you can, so that people feel they are estimating, rather than merely guessing. If the clock *can* be heard ticking in the box, charge more per guess on each succeeding day of the competition.

Cost: Low
Organisation: Simple
Profit: Low

Date tried	
Target profit	£
Profit (actual)	£

Very successful   worthwhile   unsuccessful

Notes/Comments

YEARBOOK

This activity appeals to the nostalgia – and the vanity – that is to be found in most of us at least some of the time. Basically, an illustrated book is produced to show the work and achievements of your organisation, together with photographs of *all* the personnel involved. (This last bit is of extreme importance to the success of the venture. John Smith is several times more likely to buy a copy, even at £5 or £10, if he actually appears on one of the pages.)

'Limited edition' is a phrase that can sound appealing. Bear in mind, though, that what you have is a limited clientèle, so precise market research is important. Also, unless you happen to have in your group some good photographers, creative designers, printers *et al.*, you will be advised to use a company that specialises in this type of work (see Section 6: *Useful Addresses*).

Cost: High
Organisation: Considerable
Profit: Moderate

Date tried	
Target profit	£
Profit (actual)	£

Very successful   **worthwhile**   **unsuccessful**

Notes/Comments

Section 2
30 Ideas for Your Fête

Your fête is in your own hands! Here are thirty ideas – some old, some more recent, some fairly standard such as stalls and sideshows, others more unusual – for you to consider in planning a fête or fair. The underlined activities are particularly recommended.

As well as these ideas, there are, of course, good old friends like tombola, bingo, bagatelle, bowling for a pig, bottle stalls . . . and many more.

Apple Bobbing

Old-fashioned, messy and lots of fun, this needs only a large bowl or bucket of water and a plentiful supply of apples, water and towels. Contestants win an apple simply (?) by removing it from the water using only their teeth.

Assault Course

A net, box, tyres, a bench . . . there is no need for very elaborate equipment. Time the competitors and offer a prize for whoever can complete the course in the best time.

Balloon Launch

Each participant fills in a standard form (name, address, telephone number, message . . .) which invites the finder of the balloon to be in contact. The balloon is then launched on its journey.

Beat the Goalie

You don't particularly need a well-known goalkeeper, but if you are offering a prize for each goal scored you will naturally need someone competent. Another approach is to offer one prize for the best performance in beating the keeper. Consider also 'Beat the Batsman'.

Bran Tub

This is an old favourite, of course, but it does have the advantage of there being 'a prize every time'. Wrapping each item is necessary, but rather a chore.

Chess Challenge

Or draughts, or darts or any other game or activity in which you can provide a 'champion' for all-comers to challenge. If your champion is sufficiently good to be trusted, you might wish to offer a decent prize to any challenger who manages a win.

Colour Stall

If the colour you select is, say, red, everything on sale on the stall must be of that colour. Ask a group of people in your organisation to contribute ten items each. The result will be a stall that is highly attractive and eye-catching.

Cover the Quid

This is a simple idea, but it works quite well. Place a £1 coin at the bottom of a bucket of water and invite the punters to drop a 10p piece to cover it completely. It doesn't sound too difficult really, but a basic law of physics concerning the very different properties of air and water makes it much harder than you'd expect.

Crockery Smash

Quite what makes this a popular activity is not entirely clear, although hurling balls to smash pieces of old china into smithereens does perhaps have a theraputic quality. You will need a surprisingly large quantity of rubbishy old china.

Don't Make Contact!

You will probably have seen these. Batteries, an elaborately coiled piece of wire and a rod with a closed circle at the end are all that you need. The aim is to pass the rod along the wire without making contact and sounding a bell or buzzer. Some people are surprisingly good at this, so don't offer prizes!

Face-Painting	Children love to be painted with clown faces, as Red Indians, etc. You charge for providing the service. It can be linked quite well with a fancy dress contest. Don't forget to have a mirror handy.
Fishing for a Bottle	8 or 10 people fish with modified rods (with circular hoops on the end) to encircle the top of a bottle which serves as the prize. You simply have to lower the hoop over the bottle before anyone else does.
<u>Flying Fox</u>	These have become very popular in the last few years. Holding on to a handle that fits over a wire, the customer sails down the wire to be caught at the bottom by an agile helper. Use hay bales also to halt progress – and check your insurance carefully.
Guess the . . .	Guess the number of all sorts of things. Try to find an unusual and relatively untried idea, but here are a few suggestions: - sweets in a jar - pages in a book - pennies in a box - tins in a stack - length of a ball of string - peas in some pea-pods - balloons in a car - length of an audio cassette tape
<u>Human Fruit Machine</u>	Three – or preferably four – helpers simultaneously draw either a real piece of fruit or a picture card of fruit out of a box and prizes are given for specific combinations. This needs to be organised with care or you can actually lose money.
Jewellery Stall	Such are the vagaries of fashion that even those rather tired-looking, inexpensive earrings may well have an appeal. It helps if you can mix newly-made craft items with older jewellery that has been donated.
Peg Out the Washing	This simple idea makes for an entertaining test of manual dexterity. Contestants merely have to complete two challenges against the clock (a) putting pegs from a bag onto a washing line and (b) placing the same pegs back into the bag. Keep a record of the best scores and award a prize. It is best if the challenge has to be completed one-handed.
Photo-Fit	Parts of photographs of famous people are displayed in numbered order and competitors have to name as many as they can. You may also want to include one or two local people in the group with the more famous.
Pin the Card (darts)	With three throws available, the contestant has to aim for the pips on the cards (for experts) or to hit any cards and achieve as high a score as possible (for beginners).

Pony Rides	This surely needs no explanation, but it is guaranteed success if you can manage to set it up.
Popcorn Machine	Not only is popcorn a popular seller, it is entertaining to watch being made. It is possible to hire a machine, but it can be much better value to buy one. They are available (at roughly £20) from most large department stores.
Ride-On Train	You need friends at the local Railway Modellers Club for this or a suitable enthusiast who can lend a miniature ride-on train for the under-fives. They love it.
Splat the Rat	Not for the squeamish. You manufacture a yard- (metre-) long tube and drop down inside it home-made woollen 'rats'. The contestant tries to club the rat as it appears out of the end of the tube. It is all fairly mindless, rather violent fun.
Stacking Blocks	You need 18–20 of those large lightweight plastic blocks that are found in all good nurseries. With a time limit of, say, 30 seconds, the task is to stack as many in a free-standing tower as possible with prizes for reaching certain totals.
Target Golf	Quite simply, this is a miniature putting competition. Each target is given a points value and the prize goes to the overall highest scorer.
Theme Stall	For example, pigs. Models, pictures, pig-shaped sweets – everything reflects whatever you have decided on as your theme. This stall can be extremely eye-catching, so warrants a prominent place at the fête.
Treasure Island	This is quite an established competition, and can be made colourful. You construct an island and conceal the 'treasure'. The punters then place little marker flags where they think the treasure lies – a sort of tropical 'Spot the Ball'.
Whisky Draw	You sell only fifteen tickets at a price that provides 50 per cent profit, make the draw and then go round again for another bottle. Many people are not over-keen on waiting two months to find out whether they have won a prize, so this instant-reward competition can be very popular.
Wishing Well	This will not make a fortune, but can provide another vivid, eye-catching sideshow.
Word-Maker	Use sets of letters from word-games – 'Boggle' cubes are perfect for this – and challenge each contestant to roll the cubes and construct words against a time limit with a prize for the best total.

Section 3
Making Plans

Taking time over the initial planning stages will be time well spent since careful preparation for your event will ensure its success. In this section questions for you to consider, information on the legal aspects of fundraising and a page full of tips from an experienced fundraiser provide essential background to your occasion.

Ten Questions to Consider at the Planning Stage _____

How much do you *really* need to raise?

How urgently?

For what purpose?

How much specialist expertise will you require?

Where will it come from?

At what cost?

To whom?

Will this involve 'cash-flow problems'?

How could these be solved?

By whom?

This is, of course, only an example. You may wish to draw up your own list of precise questions that apply directly to the specific event you are preparing.

Five Questions to ask Yourself about your Organisation

1. Just how much stress and strain can your committee and your willing workers stand? Might you be trying to set up one (or more!) extra event in one year than is really feasible?

2. What type of programme of events, given the number, nature, skills and qualities of your members, is best suited to your organisation? Should you be looking to set up the occasional 'blockbuster' event, or would a series of less ambitious but regular and more frequent fundraisers make better sense?

3. Are you able to run one steady, ongoing fundraiser ticking away quietly in the background – weekly Bingo, perhaps – to enable you to gamble by arranging more unusual and risky fundraiser events for variety?

4. How inexperienced are the people who will be doing the work to set up the event? How early, therefore, should the planning start (then add a few more weeks for it!)?

5. Does everyone involved know exactly what he or she and all the others are meant to be doing? Whose job is it to tell them?

Becoming a Charity

Why Do it?
There are several reasons for seeking charity status, most of them to do with money.

- You become eligible for various forms of tax exemption: for example, Income Tax, Corporation Tax, Capital Gains Tax, Capital Transfer Tax, Stamp Duty on property transfer. All of these could be advantageous to your group as a charity. Some may not apply in your case, but even if only one does, consider applying.

- Rates reduction: it may be a 80 per cent reduction, but could be even more, since there is an element of local discretion.

- Receiving help from other charities: support from other organisations is far more likely if you are a registered charity. In many communities the local Mayor is able to nominate one or two worthy causes for his or her year of office. As a charity, your chances of being selected increase considerably.

- The public image of the group: interest in your organisation and a general willingness to work on your behalf can only increase if you are accepted for charitable status.

Where Do I Find Out More?
Fundraising and Grant Aid by A. Darnborough and D. Kinrade (Woodhead-Faulkner)
ISBN 0 85941 075 7

Advertising by Charities edited by K. Burnett (Directory of Social Change)
ISBN 0 907 164 19 6

Leaving Money to Charity by M. Norton (Directory of Social Change)
ISBN 0 907 164 12 9

Raising Money from Industry edited by M. Norton (Directory of Social Change)
ISBN 0 907 164 05 6

Voluntary Organisations and the Media by M. Jones (NVCO)
ISBN 0 7199 1120 6

Starting a Charity (reference No. CC 21) (Charity Commission) – see Section 6: *Useful Addresses*)

Fundraising and the law

A definition of what a charity actually is can be found elsewhere in this guide, and information has already been given in this section about why it is worth seeking charitable status. Whether or not you do this, there are several extremely important points to bear in mind regarding the legal aspects of fundraising.

There are a number of issues that relate to children. It is an offence to allow a child under the age of 14 to be in a bar. At sixteen a child can legally buy tickets in a registered public lottery, fireworks, and consume certain types of alcohol in the restaurant section of a public house. Only at the age of 18 is it legal to buy or drink alcohol in a bar or to place bets. It is essential that you understand and abide by these regulations or you could fall foul of the law while carrying out several fundraisers suggested in this book.

Some of the traps are fairly obvious and can be pre-empted through good planning. For instance, where you plan to sell food at an event you should note that a local authority may require you to obtain a licence, whilst the sale of alcoholic drinks always requires a licence; (do not believe that the practice of selling a biscuit or a small cube of cheese for £2.50 and 'giving away' a bottle of wine with it because you do not hold a drinks licence is a reasonable or supportable device in law). Obviously you should make appropriate enquiries at an early stage.

Where an event is staged at premises other than a private dwellinghouse, you should ask your local fire authority whether a fire certificate is needed for those premises.

For some events such as plays, concerts, public dancing and music and so on, you will need to possess a public entertainments licence. This can be obtained on an annual or an occasional basis, but you will need to apply at least 28 days in advance to the local authority. The actual rates charged are fixed locally. A licence will not be required for film exhibitions at specific premises which are used only occasionally and exceptionally (and in any event on not more than six days in any calendar year) for such purposes, provided written notice of the event is given to the local licensing authority, the police and the local fire authority not less than seven days before he event and general safety regulations are observed. Conditions may be imposed by the local licensing authority.

Musical performances, theatrical productions, sound recordings, video films, etc are protected by copyright laws and will require you to contact the appropriate licensing authority (such as the Performing Rights Society, Phonographic Performance Ltd, Video Performance Ltd, etc) and pay royalties. The costs that are involved here are sufficiently high for them to feature in your planning of expenses.

Events involving betting, lotteries and gaming are subject to extremely complicated regulations which are beyond the scope of a guide of this kind. In general terms you should be able to hold entertainment events such as lotteries and bingo games at a bazaar or fete without the need to apply for a licence. You should also be able to hold lotteries, bingo games, whist drives, etc as events in their own right provided regulations concerning the amount of entrance fees charged and the total value of prizes distributed are observed. In both cases all proceeds, after deducting certain expenses, must be devoted to purposes other than for private gain, not only to ensure that the event is legal, but also to avoid any relevant tax or duty becoming payable.

If there is any possibility of your event causing noise and nuisance to others – discos, of course, are the most obvious example – the Local Environmental Health Department and the police may be able to advise you. Bear in mind that` it is far better when complaints are lodged to have tried before the event to avoid nuisance.

The law on house-to-house collections states that they must be authorised by the local licensing authority. Details of the precise location of the collection will be required and also the date or dates, the purpose and the promoter's name. If you are refused permission – and because of the number of people applying you may be – you do have the right to appeal to the Home Office. The law requires that collectors of money shall be 'fit and proper persons' for doing so. Each collector must display a badge and carry a certificate or letter of authority from the organiser. Each collecting box must be sealed. Similar regulations exist in relation to street collections.

Finally, you need to note that where you have named a charity or specific purpose for a collection or a fundraising event, it is a breach of civil law to use the money raised in any other way.

Accounts

Planning a Checklist

FACTORS TO CONSIDER	APPROX COST	NOTES
Publicity – Press		Try to develop a personal contact with the local press and radio staff.
– Radio/TV		"What's on" columns and radio/TV promotions are generally done free of charge.
– Posters		Take close note of other people's posters, handbills, etc. Yours need to be more eye catching than theirs.
Fees payable – Celebrity		"Celebrities" - think carefully: that nationally known writer of books will probably attract fewer extra visitors than the man who does the weather forecast on local television.
– Hire of premises		Premises: School halls are reasonably good value. An excellent hall of good size can cost as little as £10 per hour to hire.
– Drinks licence		Apply in plenty of time!
– Lottery licence		Apply in plenty of time!

FACTORS TO CONSIDER	APPROX COST	NOTES
Catering Costs – Food		Contributed food?
– Drink		Always offer an alternative to alcohol.
Ancillary Items – Stationery (including stamps)		
– Prizes		Contributed prizes?
– Tickets		

1. RECEIPTS

DATE	RECEIVED FROM	BANK INTEREST	COVENANTS	DONATIONS	FUND-RAISING EVENTS	RECYCLING	REFRESH-MENTS	SALES	GENERAL	TOTAL
1/1/91	Balance b/f									176.45
14/1/91	Auction				947.30					1123.75
"							64.18			1187.93
27/1/91	Parish Council			100.00						1287.93
15/2/91	Bags							272.00		1559.93
1/3/91			150.00							1709.93
22/3/91	Craft Fair				341.10					2051.03
"							104.25			2155.28
19/4/91	Dinner Dance				644.00					2799.28
22/5/91						35.00				2834.28
1/6/91		42.40								2876.68
		42.40	150.00	100.00	1932.40	35.00	168.43	272.00	-	

You will be able to operate to a maximum of about 10–12 different headings, the remainder to be covered by the 'General' column. Careful analysis of these sheets over a period of time should enable you to determine the relative success of the group's various activities. Here there are signs that little is raised through donations and that the re-cycling, although desirable environmentally, is not raising significant sums.

During this five-month period the group raised just over £2700. This should now be compared to past performances and the appropriate conclusions drawn.

2. PAYMENTS

DATE/EVENT	PAID TO	CHEQUE NO.	BAGS CO.	FOOD & DRINK	HIRE OF PREMISES	OTHER	VAT	TOTAL	TOTAL + VAT
14/1/91 (Auction)	Megastore Cash & Carry	200010		28.40			–	28.40	28.40
	Meadshire C. C	200011			125.00		18.75	153.40	172.15
1/3/91	Bulkybag Plc	200012	375.00				56.25	528.40	603.40
22.3.91 (Craft Fair)	Megastore Cash & Carry	200013		45.86			–	574.26	649.26
	Meadshire C. C.	200014			125.00		18.75	699.26	793.01
19/4/91 (Dinner Dance)	'Fancifood Caterers'	200015		395.00			59.25	1094.26	1247.26
	Meadshire C. C.	200016			175.00	–	26.25	1269.26	1448.51
			375.00	469.26	425.00		179.25	£1269.26	£1448.51

Set alongside the Receipts details, this sheet offers several indications, although the evidence is not yet conclusive:

i) The bag-selling project is not quote as flourishing as it appeared. Quite large stocks have to be kept and the income is modest.

ii) The group is having to pay out large sums for hall hire. Might the time come when renting your own premises would be preferable?

iii) The overheads for the Dinner Dance make it not quite as profitable as it seemed.

iv) The high costs in the Food and Drink column are distorted by the catering cost of the Dinner Dance. Profits in refreshments are otherwise running at around 130%!

A Quick Guide to Insurance

The golden rule is: don't leave things to chance. Any event involving the general public will require you to look at the insurance which is essential to your event. The following points are also to be borne in mind:

1.   Check carefully to ensure that you are adequately covered for:
     - personal accident
     - public liability
     - loss or damage to property/equipment

2.   Group members need to check their individual insurance policies. For example, are they covered to transport people and goods in connection with the event?

3.   You may decide to take out additional cover against, for instance, bad weather ruining everything. 'In the village hall if wet' sounds fair enough, but would it really be feasible? It is known as 'pluvius insurance'.

4.   You may well be eligible for cover through membership of some other organisation. An example would be a school PTA, which can join the National Federation of PTAs and obtain insurance cover.

A Page Full of Tips

1. What you decide to call the event can be important. A 'Nearly New Sale' can sound more worth visiting than a Jumble Sale and why not call it a *Grand* Auction?

2. If running a sponsored event, make sure you number the sponsor cards and keep close track of where they all go. Otherwise, in the wrong hands they can be misused and never seen by you, the organiser, again.

3. When running a Draw, try to have one really big, attractive prize and a maximum of around a dozen other prizes. It is not a great pleasure to most people to wait around while the winning ticket is drawn for yet another bottle of British Sherry.

4. For major fairs and fêtes, plan the event more or less the whole year round if you want to keep your committee together, then immediately give them the next challenge. It is far easier to keep the momentum going than to stop and start.

5. Keep a file of your previous press adverts, posters, etc. It will save a great deal of effort the next time. It makes particular sense if you have reason to believe you got the publicity right the last time.

6. Rather than operating a standard policy for pluvial (wet weather) insurance, look to make the logical decision each time. Take into consideration the factors that apply – how critical a downpour would be for that event, the ready availability of an alternative indoor venue, the sort of summer it is proving to be, the long-range forecast, etc.

7. Consider seriously whether to purchase any of the equipment fundraisers need instead of hiring each time. You can recoup your money rapidly on a decent P.A. system, a badge-maker and games of fête equipment, while it may also be in your interest to buy at least some of the following: spiral binder, photocopier (small), laminator, Bingo equipment, coffee-maker, projector, etc.

8. Respond to the changing times and use the free publicity the media can sometimes provide. There are various possibilities – a quiz based on a currently popular format or a fancy dress event related to everybody's favourite 'TV soap' for example.

9. Try hard to obtain a major sponsor who will offer significant support in the form of hard cash or materials. All of the rest then becomes merely performance – and fun.

10. In preparing events you will often find yourself needing odd items like a teddy bear costume or a large inflatable elephant. Don't forget how useful the 'Yellow Pages' can be in helping you to track down these unlikely items.

11. If you want someone to open the event, but cannot afford an expensive 'celebrity' consider organising an event like a May Queen competition or to find a Queen of Hearts, the best Mad Hatter, etc. The winner can then carry out the opening ceremony at no cost to you.

Sideshows and Stalls ─────────────────────────────

It is possible to obtain all the items you are likely to need for a good range of stalls from any one of several firms that specialise in this area. For example, Baker Ross currently provide the following:

a football tombola   giant card game
other sports tombolas   raffle tickets
several *other* tombolas!   scratch-cards
punchboards   balloons
Bingo equipment   search cards ('Where's the treasure?' etc.)
collecting boxes   ducks for a duck race
darts game   roll-a-coin equipment
spot the ball   fishing and hoopla games
party packs   spin the arrow

Here, though, are just two words of advice:

• look carefully at the various items on offer. One competition can be far less profitable than the next, for the terms of the deal vary greatly;

• do try to avoid games in which children are involved and the odds against winning that football, teddy bear or whatever are poor. You should not countenance the sight of young children failing to win and going away disappointed or tearful.

Section 4

Publicity

Far from being the inquisitive irritation that we may think the Press to be, journalists can prove an enormous asset to most fundraising occasions. This section explains why, and provides hints on writing the press release and newspaper advertisement which might boost the attendance of your event beyond your wildest expectations!

Contacts with the Press

Rest assured, the press will come to you quickly enough if your marquee burns down or the treasurer runs off with the cash-box. However, you will wish to contact them before the event as part of the publicity programme and afterwards with the principal aim of acknowledging support given and work done by members of your organisation.

A skilfully-worded news article or press release can reduce considerably your bill for publicity. If it sounds like news and is presented in an efficient fashion, your local newspaper is highly likely to use the copy you provide for them, very possibly without any alterations. Do check the style of the newspaper in question so you can tune in to it. A polite covering letter is also recommended. Best of all, see if you can make personal contact with one or two local reporters and treat them well if they visit on the day for more information or photographs. If you do send pictures with your press release, make sure they are in black and white rather than colour. Time and trouble taken to establish good relations with the press should never be regarded as time wasted: it can bring great dividends.

The pack of copyright-free master sheets that accompanies this book includes two press release example pages for your use.

Newspaper and Magazine Advertisements _____

The first very important rule is: don't be verbose. You are after all paying for that space by the column inch (centimetre), so those additional four sentences will cost you more, and if the result is a jumbled, confusing, less interesting advertisement they may actually detract from the effectiveness of your message. Keep it simple, therefore.

Rule number two is to make sure you produce something that is . . .

EYECATCHING!

Your event may be one of as many as thirty or forty advertised on the same page, so you must do battle for your share of the reader's attention. The most straightforward way to do this is not by over-crowding the space you have bought. The basic details of time, place, the event itself and possibly one or two of the main attractions with plenty of space around them will draw more attention than a mass of detail and no space.

It is generally worth putting your advertisement inside a frame, even a very basic one. Most newspapers will accept framed advertisements, but they may insist that they do the framing themselves. This is worth checking before and not after someone in your organisation has spent long hours of careful work! Note also that there may be an extra charge for setting up your own prepared artwork, since a plate must be made. If you are happy to have them set it, their own plates will be used and you could save on each of your advertisements.

If you can afford to buy the extra space, you may wish to attract more attention by using something rather more dramatic. Beware, though. The cost of extensive display advertising is now quite high, so check carefully at the time of planning publicity, not after what proves to be highly expensive copy is ready to go.

Section 5
Fundraising in Schools

It is a sign of our times that fundraising in schools has become crucial to their well-being. There are a great many fundraising activities given in this book which are highly successful in the school situation. This section presents these and other ideas suitable for schools alone, as well as giving the main points from a very useful pamphlet on the subject.

Fundraising in Schools

In recent years, PTAs and even some governing bodies in our schools have become more involved in fundraising activities to advance the work of the school. If the school in question is a maintained, or state school, it is essential that such efforts are directed only towards obtaining 'luxuries', those additional items that are of considerable value to the school, but which cannot in all honesty be expected out of the basic delegated budget. Even after the introduction of Local Management of Schools (LMS), a system that through an unsatisfactory formula has left many schools significantly under-funded, you will create a host of problems for yourselves if you strive hard to raise extra money for basic items of provision. To put it bluntly, you run the risk of disguising the unreasonable inadequacy of the funding of our schools.

When you are preparing a fundraising event, try to ensure that there is agreement in advance about how the money will be used. Make this generally known as part of the pre-event publicity. Whether you need a five-figure sum for, say, a minibus or only a three-figure total for perhaps some display screens or magazine subscriptions for the library, it is bound to bring a better response if people are aware of what their efforts and money will provide.

Many of the main points to be borne in mind when fundraising for schools are covered in *Fundraising in Schools*, a document published by the Institute of Charity Fundraising Managers. This very helpful pamphlet attempts to lay down a clear-cut code of practice. It opens by stating the ICFM policy, namely that children should be offered a 'positive opportunity for involvement in helping others by raising funds. Trust, it states, should be at the heart of fundraising so that, while children should be given clear instructions regarding the payment of sponsorship money, they should also be as far as possible put 'on his or her honour to pay all the money raised'. (*Author's note*: This does not conflict with advice given on p.127 to keep a check on sponsorship forms issued simply out of concern for efficiency.)

Talks when they are given should be both educational and non-political and appropriate to the age group of the children. The headteacher's approach to school charity work should be accorded with. His or her approval, even if through a designated colleague, should be received for what is carried out before contact is made with children in and near the school.

The pamphlet then goes on to list safeguards for children. These include warnings to be given regarding approaching strangers for money and that door-knocking for money is against the law. The parents, the pamphlet states, should be made aware that only friends and relatives should be approached for sponsorship and discussion with the child should indicate clearly who is and is not a potentially suitable sponsor. An authorised adult is an important pre-requisite to fundraising activities and for under-sixteens' it should be for the parents to decide whether or not a child may take part in a fundraising event'.

Where the organisation of an event is concerned, the point is made that using incentives for rewards to encourage individual efforts is seen as a very sensitive issue, and the greatest care needs to be exercised in offering them to children. Token gifts, if awarded, should be available to all and ideally will encourage participants to reflect on the work of the charity concerned. If monetary rewards are given, the system should be tightly regulated and the headteacher's full approval must be obtained. Particular care is needed, the pamphlet stresses, with the offer of incentives to the under-sevens. For a sponsored event the maximum sum that might be achieved by the participant must be clearly defined.

All fundraising materials, ICFM says, 'should be written in clear, simple language. From time to time special material may need to be prepared for those who do not have English as their mother tongue, subject to the headteacher's advice.'

The fourth section of the pamphlet offers advice to the event organiser. Key points include full discussion with the headteacher, the need to set a time limit for events and to minimise the inconvenience to school staff. The appropriateness of courtesy is also pointed out, through a reminder that all the appropriate parties should be thanked for their involvement.

General points made include advice on how to deal with complaints or criticism and the need to train participating staff 'on a continuing basis on every aspect of their work'. In addition, legal points regarding street and house-to-house collections and the obtaining of a licence are made.

The rest of the pamphlet states the actual ICFM Code of Conduct under these headings:

- Professional Conduct
- Injury to Others
- Honesty
- Professional Competence
- Conflict of Interests
- Confidentiality

Where the enforcement of the Code is concerned, the document states 'it is the duty of all members to assist the Institute in implementing and enforcing the Code and they will be supported by the Institute for so doing.'

Ideas for Schools

Many of the ideas for fundraising activities given in Section 1 of this book are highly appropriate for use in schools as either separate events or at your fête. Here is a list of some relevant ideas from Section 1:

Badges
Bags
Bouncing
Cards and Notelets
Christmas Cards
Christmas Decorations
Cookery Book
Crazes
Fill the Tube!
Fortune-telling
Games Evening
Hobbies Day/Hobbies Fair
'It's a Knockout'
Joke Books
Mugs
Nametapes
Non-uniform Day
Photographs
Quiz Booklets
Quiz Supper
Recycling
Schoolgoal
Shoeshine
Stickers
Sunflower Growing
Talent Show
T-shirts/ Sweatshirts, etc.
Toy Making

As well as these ideas, what about the following projects?

- Why not sell pupils' art-work?

- What about running a school shop? An unwanted or under-used locker or cloakroom area might be converted quite cheaply for a shop opening each day for an hour or two to sell uniform (you could include good-quality second-hand items), stationery, cards, badges, snacks and so on.

- Have you the storage facility to enable you to make recycling a major activity at the school (see RECYCLING)?

- Could you sell a good number of shoulder bags, some of them carrying the school name and/or crest (see BAGS)?

- Is there on the site a suitable venue for a day nursery to include some places made available to local companies for their employees?

- Did you know that the NCPTA runs a trust to provide additional books for school libraries? Your school might be eligible for as many as one book per pupil in the school free of charge.

- Have you considered using a group of young offenders to decorate parts of the school as their community service sentence? With materials provided, proper supervision and some basic instruction they could not only do you a good job, but also save the school huge amounts in labour costs.

- Do you know about 'Schoolplan'? This is a fundraising idea promoted through the NAHT Management Services company, whereby the school runs a mail-order service using their own catalogue with discounts available as a proportion of sales. Details of how to find out more are provided in Section 6: *Useful Addresses*.

- Are you considering – or should you consider – obtaining charitable status for your PTA? The NCPTA will provide, free of charge, a copy of the Home-School Association Model Constitution and *Helping Hand* an informative leaflet on seeking charitable status (see Section 6: *Useful Addresses*).

Section 6
Useful Addresses

It's time to call in the professionals! This section contains a list in alphabetical order of useful contacts. The appearance of any particular company on the list should not, however, be taken as a recommendation or a guarantee of its excellence – you will have to check that for yourself! Add in the names of companies you use for your own future reference.

Useful Addresses ──────────────

Advice on Advertising
Advertising Standards Authority
Department X
Brook House
Torrington Place
London
WC1E 7HN

Badges/Buttons
(Your own designs possible – a minimum
quantity of 150 pieces)

Badges Plus
9–11 Vittoria Street
Birmingham
B1 3ND
Tel. (021) 236 1612

The London Badge and Button Co. Ltd
3 Duke of York Street
Jermyn Street
St James's
London
SW1Y 6JP
Tel. (071) 321 0474

London Emblem Plc
(See under Keyrings)

Renamel Badges Ltd.
Cumberland Road
Stanmore
Middx
HA7 1QH
Tel. (081) 204 9522-4

Universal Button Co. Ltd
10–12 Witan Street
Bethnal Green
London E2 6JX
Tel. (071) 739 5750
(Also pens, combs, a
range of 'novelty items')

Westfield Advertising
Specialities Ltd

Helena Street
Birmingham
B1 2RJ
Tel. (021) 233 1671
Fax (021) 236 4121

Balloons and Kites
The Kite & Balloon Company
The Old Church
160 Eardley Road
London
SW16 5TG
Tel. (081) 679 8844

Bouncing
'Mr Bounce'
FREEPOST
Watlington
Oxford
OX9 5BR
(Uses a large inflatable dragon)

Cards/Wrapping Paper
Club Centre Ltd
Church Bridge
Accrington
Lancs.
BB5 4EN
(Offers 25% profits)

Hall Green Cards
Hall Green
Wakefield
West Yorks.
WF4 3JT
(50% offered on all sales)

Christmas Cards
EM Designs
84 Pound Road
East Peckham
Nr Tonbridge
Kent TN12 5BJ
(From your own designs)
Tel. 0622 071 303

'Come Racing' Nights
Beneficial Arts UK Ltd
Dept 38
31 Elkstone Road
London
W10 5NT
Tel. (081) 969 6588

Covenanting
Craigmyle & Co.
Fundraising Consultants
The Grove
Harpenden
Herts.
AL5 1AH
Tel. Harpenden (0582) 762441

Craft Fair
Start-a-Craft
6 Manor Road
Hatfield
Herts.
AL10 9LN

Diaries
Customer Services Dept
Charles Letts & Co. Ltd
Thornybank Industrial Estate
Dalkeith
Midlothian
Scotland
EH22 2NE
(Discount rate for schools/colleges only)

Draw Tickets
Ha'penny Press
Caxton House
Holbrook
Ipswich
Suffolk
IP9 2QS
Tel. (0473) 328400

Fabric Printing
Stuart Morris Textiles
Hand Printed Fabrics
The Rose Chapel Print Studio
George Street

Hadleigh
Suffolk
IP7 5BT
Tel. Hadleigh (0473) 824212
(Promotional products, tea towels T-shirts and sweatshirts)

See also: T-shirts and sweatshirts

Fireworks (Display Kits)
Pains Fireworks
Old Chalkpit
Whiteparish
Wilts.
Tel. (0794) 884040
(Professional and kit displays)

Reverend Lancaster
Kimbolton Fireworks
7 High Street
Kimbolton
Huntingdon
Cambs.
PE18 08B

Skyfires
Westcott
Old Salisbury Road
Abbotts Ann
Andover
Hampshire
SP11 7NH
Tel. (0264) 710784

Food Hampers
Family Hampers
Fund Raising Club
FREEPOST
Temple House
Ring Road
Seacroft
Leeds
West Yorks.
LS14 1YT

Fund-Raising Advice
Charity Solutions

7 Acacia Road
London
NW8 6AB
Tel. (081) 313 3662

Information on tax relief on gifts can be obtained from any Tax Office or Tax Enquiry Centre, or from the Inland Revenue's Claims Branch (Charity Divsion) at:
St John's House
Merton Road
Bootle
Merseyside
L69 9EJ

Trinity Park House
South Trinity Road
Edinburgh
EH5 3SD

General
The Charity Commission
St Albans House
57–60 Haymarket
London
SW1Y 4QX
Tel. (071) 210 3000

General – 25% profit guaranteed
Ace Cards and Gifts
Miller Street
Preston
Lancs
PR1 4WR

Baker Ross Limited
Unit 53
Milmead Industrial Estate
Mill Mead Road
Tottenham
London
N17 9ND

Webb Ivory
FREEPOST
Primrose Hill
Preston

Lancs
PR1 4WU

Ice Cream, Yogurts, Milk Shakes
Taylor Freezer (UK) Plc
Denmark House
Old Bath Road
Twyford
Berks.
RG10 8BR

Keyrings
London Emblem PLC
Emblem House
Blenheim Road
Longmead Industrial Estate
Epsom
Surrey
KT19 9AP
Tel. Epsom (0372) 745433

Laminating/Ring-binding
Muromail
Murographics Ltd
Gazelle Road
Oldmixon
Weston-Super-Mare
Avon
BS24 9EW
Tel. (0934) 636393 or
(0800) 378193

Live Music
Performing Right Society
29-33 Berners Street
London
W1P 4AA
Tel. (071) 580 5544

Lotteries
Lotteries and Gaming: Voluntary Organisations and the Law
(published by National Council for Voluntary Organisations)
Available from:
MacDonald & Evans Distribution Services
Estover Road

Plymouth
Devon
PL6 7PZ

Mugs
(Custom printed for advertising purposes or fundraisers. Prices start at around £1 + VAT)

Berkshire China Co. Ltd
298 King Street
Fenton
Stoke-on-Trent
Staffs.
ST4 3EN
Tel. (0782) 311447

Denmead Pottery and Glassworks
Parklands Business Park
Forest Road
Denmead
Hants.
Tel. (0705) 261945

Keramicos
Unit 5
Lumsdale Mill
Lower Lumsdale
Matlock
Derbys.
DE 4 5EX
Tel. (0629) 580033

Laughame Pottery
Kingstreet
Langhame
Dyfed
SA33 4RY
Tel. (0994)427476

Name Tapes
Permark Name Tapes
Permark House
1 Station Grove
Wembley
Middx
HA0 4AH
Tel. (081) 903 4544

The National Weaving Company
34 Tresham Road
Orton Southgate
Peterborough
PE2 0SG
Tel. (0733) 237007

Novelties and Accessories
Barnums Carnival Novelties
67 Hammersmith Road
London
W14 8UZ
Tel. (071) 602 1211

Dodd Anderson Ltd
21 Denmark Street
Heaton
Newcastle-upon-Tyne
NE6 2XE

Fête & Fayre Enterprises Ltd
6-7 The Parade
Pound Street
Carshalton
Surrey
SM5 3PG
Tel. (081) 647 2964
(Wide range)

Goldmark Gifts Ltd
59 Oak Grove
London
NW2 3NR
Tel. (081) 452 0737
(Colour catalogue available)

Goldpress
4 Meadowlands
Scholes
Cleckheaton
West Yorks.
BD19 6HB
Tel. (0274) 878488
('express service')

Miller Fundraising
FREEPOST

Adelaide Street
Preston
Lancs
PR1 4WY

Northern Novelties Pencils Ltd
Spencer House
18 Napier Road
Bradford
BD3 8BT
Tel. (0274) 664665

Nye's Novelties
173 Cambridge Road
Hitchin
Herts.
Tel. (0462) 32346

Peeks of Bournemouth Ltd
Riverside Lane
Tuckton
Bournemouth
Hants.
BH6 3LD
Tel. (0202) 417777

Pens
Names stamped
Abbey Wholesale Supply
974 and 976 London Road
Trent Vale
Stoke-on-Trent
Staffs.
ST4 5NX

Personalised Goods
FP Products
FREEPOST, Dept F
21 Marchwood Grove
Clayton
Bradford
BD14 6BR
Tel. (0274) 815110

Handmade Books
FREEPOST
37 Chatsworth Road

Surrey
CR9 9EN
Tel. (081) 886 2352
*(Books that feature the child and
his/her name in the story)*

Insignia Ltd
1 – 6 Chalice Close
Lavender Vale
Wallington
Surrey
SM6 9QS
(081) 669 7192

Raydor Publicity Printing
'Appledore'
Stretton Heath
Halfway House
Shrewsbury
Salop.
SY5 9QQ
Tel. (0743) 821258

Westfield
Advertising Specialities
Westfield House
Helena Street
Birmingham
B1 2RJ
Tel. (021) 233 1671

Winston Promotions Ltd
Unit 3
Forest Industrial Park
Forest Road
Ilford
Essex
IG6 3HL
Tel. (081) 501 3939

Poster Club
Plaistow Pictorial
Church House
Church Street
London
E15 3JA
Tel. (081) 534 8833

Recorded Music
Mechanical-Copyright
Protection Society
General Licensing Department
41 Streatham High Road
London
SW16 1ER
Tel. (081) 769 4400

Recycling
Cash-A-Can HQ
Goldsmith Avenue
Southsea
Hants.
PO4 8QX
Tel. (0705) 739132

D.J.K. Packaging Ltd
Unit 8, Rawcliff House
Heworth Road
Maidenhead
Berkshire
SC6 1AP
(Produce a can crusher)

Roll-A-Dice
Hamilton & Wellard Underwriting Agency
69/71 Great Eastern Street
London
EC2A 3HU
Tel. (071) 739 4300

School Activities
Schoolgoal
Haydock High School
Clipsley Lane
Haydock
St Helens
WA11 OJG

Schoolplan
Freepost
139 Clapham Road
London
SW99 OHR
*Mail order (discount to schools), run by NAHT
Management Development Services Ltd*

School Magazines
Plaistow Press Magazines
Church House
Church Street
Stratford
London
E15 3JA
Tel. (081) 534 8833

Schoolwear (Mail Order)
Kay's – in partnership with:
Robert Fearnley-Whittingstall
Schoolwear Consortium Ltd
Merlin Haven House
Wotton-under-Edge
Glos.
GL12 7BA
Tel. (0453) 843655

Signs/Posters
Edprint
234 Holyhead Road
Wellington
Telford
Salop.
TF1 2DZ
Tel. (0952) 48623

Snacks (Vending)
Multisnack Ltd
Riding Hall
Halifax
West Yorks.
HX3 9XG
Tel. (0422) 348444

Stickers *(and other items)*
Libra Graphics Ltd
Dewsbury Mills
Dewsbury
West Yorks.
WF12 9QE
Tel. Dewsbury (0924) 456361/2
Fax 0924 461632

Tape the Show!
Wizard Video Productions
Petworth Road
Witley
Surrey
GU8 5LK
Tel. (0428) 682896

Tea Towels
Lorna Wiles Textiles (HP)
Wesley Yard
Newquay
Cornwall
TR7 1LB
Tel. (0637) 876840
(your design printed)

Teddies *(wearing T-shirts!)*
Insignia Ltd
1 – 6 Chalice Close
Lavender Vale
Wallington
Surrey
SM6 9QS

T-Shirts and Sweatshirts
BCT-Shirts
Leisure-wear Suppliers
62 – 64 Queen's Circus
Battersea
London SW8
Tel. (071) 622 3589

Interprint
Dale Street
Craven Arms
Shropshire.
SY7 9NY
(0588) 673444

Fundraising Officer
Toye, Kenning & Spencer
19 – 21 Great Queen Street
London
WC2B 5BE
Tel. (071) 242 0471

Sprintprint
(Dept EE) Printing House
Westmead Industrial Estate
Westmead Drive
Swindon
Wilts.
SN5 7YT
Tel. (0793) 695766

Star Screen
Co-op building
Walbottle
Tyne and Wear
NE15 9RY
Tel. (091) 229 0226

Thompson Print Ltd
5 Otterwood Square
Martland Mill
Wigan
Lancs.
WN5 0LF
Tel. (0942) 227519

Tombola
V. Webster Ltd
Brinell Way
Hafreys Estate
Gt Yarmouth
Norfolk
NR31 0LU
Tel. (0493) 651111

Year Books
John Catt Ltd
Great Glemham
Saxmundham
Suffolk
IP17 2DH

Jostens School Services
Anthony R. Percival
Regional Manager
8 Luard Court
Havant
Hants.
PO9 2TN

Section 7

Post-mortem Time

As well as 'How much did we make?' there are other questions that should be asked immediately after your event. This section discusses these and helps you pinpoint what aspects were particularly successful and where improvements can be made next time.

How Did We Do?

Understandably, that is the question on people's lips after the event has finished. For a large event the sheer counting of the money may take quite a while, so you should try to provide some form of preliminary balance sheet at the very first opportunity. People who have given time and energy have a right to know. You can always make it clear that these accounts are not final. Below, you will find a sample sheet of this kind from a Christmas Bazaar that raised close to £2000:

Preliminary Figures Accounts *Not* Final

	Receipts	Expenses	Profit
Draw	£671.20	£68.00	£603.20
Bottle Stall	£218.94		£218.94
Bottles Galore	£181.55		£181.55
Cocktail Bar and Cards	£131.23		£131.23
Bric-a-brac	£113.27		£113.27
Craft	£112.76		£112.76
Coffee Bar	£93.68		£93.68
Popcorn and Sweets	£75.55		£75.55
Jewellery	£58.41		£58.41
Books	£56.10		£56.10
Silent Auction	£53.10		£53.10
Calendars	£34.60		£34.60
Christmas Decorations	£33.21		£33.21
Lucky Dip	£24.34		£24.34
Computers	£22.50		£22.50
Snooker/Darts	£20.45		£20.45
Whiskey Raffle	£20.00		£20.00
Plants	£17.00		£17.00
Cover the Quid	£15.28		£15.28
Christmas Tree	£5.00		£5.00
Pegs on Line	£3.70		£3.70
Pennies in a Jar	£3.30		£3.30
Chess Challenge	£0.89		£0.89
TOTAL	£1,966.06	£68.00	£1,898.06

A warm THANK YOU to all who helped to raise this very useful sum! Please note that some further expenses have yet to be deducted.

Just How Organised is Your Organisation?

Use the check-list below to assess whether your group is efficient enough to carry out effective fundraising. If you score fewer than ten YES answers it suggests there is some room for doubt!

1. Is there a committee?   YES/NO

2. Are its meetings run to an agenda and minuted?   YES/NO

3. Is there readily available a written list of your members, their
    addresses, telephone numbers, official posts held and precise
    responsibilities?   YES/NO

4. Are proper, up-to-date accounts kept?   YES/NO

5. Are they audited?   YES/NO

6. Is there more than one authorised person able to sign cheques?   YES/NO

7. Does the group benefit from at least some of the funds gaining
    interest on deposit?   YES/NO

8. Have you considered applying for charitable status?   YES/NO

9. Does the group keep abreast of external factors (the changes in
    interest rates, E.C. changes after 1992 etc.)?   YES/NO

10. Has the group a formal constitution?   YES/NO

11. Do you have a list of useful contacts?   YES/NO

12. Do you have a secure short-term storage system for funds?   YES/NO

13. Do you know the current advertising costs locally?   YES/NO

14. Do you possess a cash and carry card?   YES/NO

15. Is someone responsible for recruiting new members?   YES/NO

Check-list 1: Why did it go so well? _____

1. Was the advance planning sufficiently in advance? YES/NO

2. Did the organisers have the necessary skills and experience? YES/NO

3. If not, was it possible to find the people needed? YES/NO

4. Was the project a reasonably original one? YES/NO

5. Was the publicity for the event adequate? YES/NO

6. Was the weather helpful? YES/NO

7. Was a harmonious atmosphere created? YES/NO

8. Was the organisation on the day efficient? YES/NO

9. Were access to the site and car parking arrangements good? YES/NO

10. Was a suitable amount of time allowed? YES/NO

11. Were people made to feel welcome? YES/NO

12. Were there sufficient helpers to clear up afterwards? YES/NO

13. Were those who helped create the event suitably thanked? YES/NO

14. Was the venue made attractive? YES/NO

15. Did it all add to the prestige/public awareness of your group? YES/NO

Check-list 2: Why did it fail? _____

1.	Were the arrangements rushed? Why?	YES/NO
2.	Were the plans altered at a late stage?	YES/NO
3.	Did it prove more complicated to organise than anticipated?	YES/NO
4.	Was it more expensive to prepare than the budget could stand?	YES/NO
5.	Was the project sufficiently unusual and appealing?	YES/NO
6.	Was there sufficient – and suitable – publicity?	YES/NO
7.	Did you generate enthusiasm in those working for the event?	YES/NO
8.	Was the weather helpful?	YES/NO
9.	Were there any avoidable last-minute problems?	YES/NO
10.	Were you unlucky with the *un*avoidable types of problem?	YES/NO
11.	Was the organisation on the day satisfactory?	YES/NO
12.	Did everyone know his or her area of responsibility?	YES/NO
13.	Were access to the site and car parking arrangements good?	YES/NO
14.	Did the event (a) over-run or (b) under-run?	YES/NO
15.	Was the venue made sufficiently attractive?	YES/NO
16.	Was it the wrong venue?	YES/NO
17.	Was enough done to make people feel welcome?	YES/NO
18.	Was the potential for financial profit over-estimated?	YES/NO
19.	Did you make enough use of the media to cover the event?	YES/NO
20.	Were there enough helpers to clear up afterwards?	YES/NO

Planning the Next Event! _____

There are many ways of using this book as you prepare a fundraising event. You could for example:

- analyse an idea that is outlined in Section 1 or Section 2.

- answer the **Ten Questions to Consider** (Section 3, page 118)

- assess the **Five Questions to ask yourself about your organisation** (Section 3, page 119)

- plan your accounts (Section 3, pages 122–123)

- draft a letter to a company (Section 6, pages138–46)

- produce a first draft of a press release (Section 4, page 130)

- frame an advertisement or poster (Section 4, page 131)

- complete one of the check-lists (Section 7, pages 149–51)

With careful planning, determination to succeed and a modicum of luck, anyone can be a successful fundraiser. May you achieve all three – and that subsequent success!